GW00818406

"Faced with new challenges of a [...] knowledge-based service economy, w[...] the odds of failure are indeed high for [...] and the real-life experience and tips [...] odds in your favour if you take these le.......... .. .., ... book with some important key messages, I recommend this to all new managers who want a lift-up in their careers."

— *Dr. N. Varaprasad, CEO*
National Library Board, Singapore

"This is a useful guide for first-time managers, and also serves as a refresher for more experienced managers who may continue to struggle with leadership challenges. It provides an important bridge between theory and practice. A must-read for any manager who wants to become an effective leader!"

— *Paul Lim, Director*
Centre for Leadership Development
Civil Service College, Singapore

"BH Tan has succeeded in creating a book of insight and practical advice for those managers embarking on their first management assignment in Asia. His unique perspective of both East and West provides a useful resource for both first-time managers and more senior experienced managers alike."

— *Andrew Stanleick, Managing Director*
L'Oreal Malaysia

"A very interesting and wise book. BH was able to put together his amazing experience in a very practical, simple and structured manner to give new managers valuable insights. This is definitely a book I will recommend to others. I will personally dip into it from time to time to look for advice for both myself and my direct reports."

— *Younes Alaoui, Vice President & General Manager*
Lafarge Concrete, South East Asia

"The author shares fundamental truths even experienced managers tend to take for granted. Highly readable. I would recommend it for all managers, not just first-time managers."

— *Susan Ho*
IFF Talent Center of Excellence, Greater Asia

"As a management educator as well as an executive coach and trainer, I recommend this not only to the first- time manager in Asia, but as a text book for MBA schools. Tan explains the essentials with clarity, reflecting his years of experience helping managers enhance their effectiveness."

— Dr. Zareen Karani Araoz, Director
Lexicon Institute of Management Education, Pune, India &
President, Managing Across Cultures, Boston USA/Pune, India

"Successful managers often forget they started from the bottom of the ladder. A kind and wise soul came along and gave them that helpful first push. BH Tan is such a soul. His insights and wisdom will guide you to widen your horizon and to scale new heights."

— Foo See Luan, Executive Coach
Founder and Past President of Singapore Chapter of International
Coach Federation and Asia Pacific Alliance of Coaches

"I have enjoyed this book greatly. I loved especially the managerial anecdotes which are all so true. BH Tan has covered almost all aspects of leadership, which is hard to find in other books. Many people will benefit from it, regardless if she is a first-time manager or an experienced one. I hope to see it changing the leadership journey of many future leaders."

— Chen Sue Cheng, Learning & Development Manager, Asia
Celestica

"A wonderful book for first-time managers but also very applicable for those who have been managing for a long time. The author combines a nice mixture of theory, practical examples, case studies and models to bring everything together. It reads easily and just makes sense. It is definitely a book that I would recommend to my clients from all over the world who are rising leaders/managers within organizations."

— Nancy Verhoeven, Executive Coach
Vincere Coaching Pte Ltd

"I wish for every new manager to have this book. If only I had it earlier in my career... It is a valuable source of best approaches to work issues, and a major practical contribution to the managerial profession."

— Leslie Chong, IT Manager, Canada

"At last, a book that I can truly recommend without hesitation to the managers and leaders I coach globally and regionally in Asia—a book that is relevant, practical, usable; a book I can ask my coachees to refer to before, during and after a coaching session; a book I wish I had when I started on my own leadership journey many years ago."
— *Su-chzeng Ong, Executive Coach and ex-senior leader of an investment bank*

"A must-read... A great foundation for getting started—whether you have just been promoted to a managerial position, or are looking for changes and improvements in your leadership style after being a leader for a long time already."
— *Jane Dmitrova, Senior Business Analyst, Netherlands*

"This book definitely deserves a place on the bookshelves of all managers, going beyond cultural differences! Not only does it serve as a good handbook for new managers, the insights and examples offer valuable reflections, for even the most experienced managers."
— *Josephine Teo, Learning for Development Director L'Oreal Asia-Pacific*

"BH has distilled his decades of executive and coaching experiences into the profound insights that underlie this comprehensive and practical guidebook for first-time managers. All first-time managers, their bosses, and senior managers who are facing challenges in leading and managing should read it! Spare 20 minutes to immerse yourself into the world of leadership, one chapter per night, and practise it the next day. Soon you would experience the profound change that emerges from the inner you!"
— *Spencer Liao, Dean TSMC College*

"It's about time for such a book. In a friendly and conversational manner, the author shows how new managers will become even more effective if they borrow from the West while looking to the East."
— *Lin Heng, Group Vice President Crop Protection, Asia Pacific, BASF*

First-Time
MANAGER
in Asia

Maximizing your success
by blending East and
West best practices

The First-Time MANAGER in Asia

Maximizing your success by blending East and West best practices | in Asia

BH TAN

Marshall Cavendish
Business

First published 2010, reprinted 2011
© Marshall Cavendish International (Asia) Private Limited

This revised edition published in 2016 by Marshall Cavendish Business
An imprint of Marshall Cavendish International
1 New Industrial Road, Singapore 536196

Other Marshall Cavendish Offices:
Marshall Cavendish Corporation. 99 White Plains Road, Tarrytown NY 10591-9001, USA • Marshall Cavendish International (Thailand) Co Ltd. 253 Asoke, 12th Flr, Sukhumvit 21 Road, Klongtoey Nua, Wattana, Bangkok 10110, Thailand • Marshall Cavendish (Malaysia) Sdn Bhd, Times Subang, Lot 46, Subang Hi-Tech Industrial Park, Batu Tiga, 40000 Shah Alam, Selangor Darul Ehsan, Malaysia.

Marshall Cavendish is a trademark of Times Publishing Limited

National Library Board Singapore Cataloguing in Publication Data
Name(s): Tan, B. H. (Boon Hock), 1953-
Title: The first-time manager in Asia : maximizing your success by blending East and West best practices / BH Tan.
Description: Second edition. I Singapore : Marshall Cavendish Business, [2016]
Identifier(s): OCN 947026645 I ISBN 978-981-47-5199-5 (paperback)
Subject(s): LCSH: Management—Asia. I Personnel management—Asia.
Classification: DDC 658.40095—dc23

Printed by NPE Print Communications Pte Ltd

To Boon Hwa, Andrea and Amelia

PREFACE

As a first time manager, you have a lot to learn. This wonderful and insightful book by executive coach and leadership consultant BH Tan will teach you what you need to know to manage well.

Learning to manage and becoming a leader isn't something that comes naturally to everyone. Just because you get that promotion you've wanted or think you deserve it doesn't mean you will automatically know what to do. It takes work, diligence, and wisdom to be successful at running a project, a team, a department, or an organization. And, that is what BH will help you with when you read *The First-Time Manager in Asia.*

In this book, the author will help you answer many of the questions that you will inevitably have, like: What challenges will you face? What skills and knowledge do you need? How do you get the most out of your team? What will be expected of you? What pitfalls should you avoid? And many more.

In grappling with the lessons that are inevitable for first-time managers, I have found that one thing is critical — the team you lead is more critical to the success of a project or organization than what you contribute as a facilitator. You are only as good as your team.

I coached a manager years ago, who eagerly accepted the challenge of a new project. He quickly involved his team in the project, and established a rigorous project management process. Each person took responsibility for creating positive synergy with cross-organizational colleagues. They regularly reported on their efforts in reaching out to their partners across the company. They kept learning from all of their colleagues — and sharing what they learned with each other. They thanked people for ideas and suggestions and followed up to ensure effective implementation.

Of all of the clients that I have ever coached, I spent the least amount of time with this manager. There seemed to be an inverse relationship between his team spending time with me and his team getting better! As a coach, this was very humbling. At the end of our project, I discussed my observations with him. I noted, "I think that I spent less time with you and your team than any team I have ever coached, yet you and your team produced the most dramatic, positive results. What should I learn from my experience?"

He thought about my question. "As a coach," he said, "you should realize that success with your clients isn't all about you. It's about the people who choose to work with you." He modestly chuckled, then continued: "In a way, I am the same. The success of my project isn't about me. It's all about the great people who are working with me." And, as a first-time manager, this will be true for you too!

In *The First-Time Manager in Asia*, BH Tan has written a book full of insights and practical advice into the subject of management that is invaluable for both first-timers and those who have been managing for a long time. As someone who has been in the field for many years, he has expanded my knowledge on the subject of management greatly with this book. For this reason I must say a very heartfelt "Thank you!" BH Tan.

Marshall Goldsmith, *New York Times* and million copy best-selling author of *MOJO* and *What Got You Here Won't Get You There*.

CONTENTS

ACKNOWLEDGEMENTS

This book has emerged from my years as a business executive and subsequently as a leadership development consultant. Many coaches, teachers and business leaders with whom I have had the privilege of working have taught me much over the years. Some of their ideas and experiences are reflected in the pages of this book. To these wise and generous people, I would like to express my deepest gratitude.

There are also many supportive clients around the world who have provided me the opportunities to test and refine the concepts and frameworks I have shared. The practical nature of this book owes much to the interesting and challenging assignments from these clients and I thank them truly.

My deepest appreciation goes to Dr. Marshall Goldsmith for writing the preface to this book. Special thanks to Dr. Brian O. Underhill who, despite his very hectic schedule, kindly agreed to write the Foreword. I would also like to extend my profound and heartfelt gratitude to my friends, colleagues and clients around the world who have read the draft of this book and offered suggestions for improvements. Despite their busy agendas, they took precious time off to give me a hand. My deepest thanks to: Lin Heng, Josephine Teo, Spencer Liao, Andrew Stanleick, Dr. N. Varaprasad, Paul Lim, Leslie Chong, Younes Alaoui, Susan Ho, Nancy Verhoeven, Foo See Luan, Chen Sue Cheng, Jane Dmitrova, Ong Su-Chzeng, Mark D'Souza, Dr. Mimi Choong, James Wong, Sandra Henson, Audrey Lee, Shereen Kaur, Geraldine Lee, Sandra Drought, Dr. Zareen Karani Araoz and Olwyn Merritt. They have all helped me improve my writing. Any shortcomings that remain are entirely my responsibility.

I am greatly indebted to my esteemed publishing team at Marshall Cavendish: Chris Newson, Violet Phoon and Lee Mei Lin who saw the potential in this book when it was just a figment of my imagination; Editor Mabelle Yeo, whose creative passion, editorial professionalism and insights I greatly value; Stephanie Pee, who is always open to new ideas, yet so disciplined in coordinating and keeping to the timelines agreed; Marketing Manager Patricia Ong and her team; illustrator Edwin Ng and designer Bernard Go. I do thank you all indeed.

Finally, my deepest love and thanks to my remarkable wife, Boon Hwa, home manager extraordinaire, and my daughters Andrea and Amelia, first-time managers at their workplace. They bring me joy every day.

FOREWORD

My first experience in "management" was a complete disaster.

I was a private school elementary teacher, in charge of music for the kindergarten through sixth grade. I had approximately six classes of different grades that I would visit during the day. What I thought would be my dream job went terribly sour.

For several years leading up to the position, I was a very successful personal piano teacher. I would teach pupils one on one. All the days that I had allocated to teaching were packed with students. I was greatly enjoying my work and earning good money.

So good at it was I that several of the parents recommended me as a teacher for their private school. I was honoured by the opportunity and intrigued with the possibilities: greater responsibility and more chances to make an impact. Plus, the money was much better. All I would have to do was more of what I did as a personal teacher, and I'd be a success in the classroom.

I couldn't have been more wrong. What got me "here", was not going to get me "there".

I began the school year as the "cool, friendly teacher", just like I did when I taught individually. I was the nice guy that all the kids liked— amiable, fun, easy-going. I would differentiate myself from the typical "old-lady stern educator-type" teacher. It would be easy. Or so I thought.

Within two weeks, I had lost total control of all my classrooms. The children were running amuck doing anything they wanted right in front of me. They would talk whenever they pleased, got up and did whatever they wished, laughed in each other's faces and even laughed at me. The kids would yell, scream, throw things and even hit each other, completely ignoring my useless threats to enforce order. I wasn't even close to completing the lessons plans I had drafted up.

I was totally miserable. I'd made a terrible mistake thinking I could make it as a school teacher. My low point came when the headmistress stormed into one of my out-of-control classrooms and yelled at the students for five minutes straight. She had heard the noise from her office and had had enough. Obviously I couldn't control the situation, so she would take charge. I'm still amazed that I made it through the rest of that year.

Today I serve as an executive coach, working with leaders of some of the world's largest companies. And I remain fascinated by what makes a good manager and leader. Having coached literally hundreds of leaders, I have decided that the transition from individual contributor to first-time manager is the hardest one to make in one's career.

I learned—the hard way—that one of the many challenges a new manager faces is how to hold others accountable. Many new leaders will try the tactic I did—that of being everyone's friend (especially if they were once peers)—only to find that to be difficult, if not impossible.

I see this in the new leaders I work with. They allow less-than-acceptable performance to go on and on. They try to say something to the offending employee, but it is usually done in a soft manner, and with no consequences, therefore allowing the employee to continue the undesirable behaviour unabated until a more experienced manager takes control of the situation.

I also meet other new managers who face a different challenge—and that is over-control. We will see this in Chapter 1 in the story of Janet, a rookie manager who tries to control all the activities of her direct reports, only to the severe frustration of all involved. She eventually leaves the company in exasperation (and, ironically, goes on to become a school teacher).

Many years ago, I coached a manager from a mobile phone handset maker who was just like Janet. She was brillant technically and educated in an Ivy League institution. As an analyst, she did all her assignments flawlessly. She was then promoted to run a small customer service division but she quickly became a relentless micromanager. It took some time (and a few people leaving) before we figured out why she couldn't let go. One day, as I questioned her, she had a magical epiphany: "I feel like if I'm not doing the work, I'm then not adding any value."

Aha! With that realization, we worked to change the way she could add value—from doing the actual work alone to getting the work done through people. I'm quite sure just that simple realization alone saved her future career at the company.

This book is an invaluable resource for all managers, especially for those transitioning from their roles as individual contributors to first-time managers. Those of us who did it on our own have learnt how tough it can be. From a coach who has done the same thing himself and worked with plenty of others to help them succeed, comes this timely gift.

By the way, as I mentioned, I did survive that year teaching, and went on to teach a second (and final) year. I quickly found a few "mentors/coaches"—seasoned teachers who showed me the ropes. They taught me that I had to immediately institute a new, consistent set of rules with the children and promptly enforce them. Once the students saw that I was serious, things started to turn around. After I had earned their respect as the authority figure, I could gradually start to play the "cool, friendly" teacher role. As BH said in Chapter 8, leaders need to exercise a blend of soft and hard power in order to be effective.

Hopefully you can learn to navigate this transition better than many of us have before you. With a resource like this book, I am confident that you are already on your way. I wish you the best of luck!

Brian O. Underhill, Ph.D.
Founder and CEO, CoachSource
Co-author of *Executive Coaching for Results:*
The Definitive Guide to Developing Organizational Leaders

INTRODUCTION

WHEN YOU BECOME A MANAGER

Why a book on the first-time manager? Isn't learning how to manage people something that comes naturally as you progress up the ladder in your career? And, frankly, looking at the managers around you, haven't these people picked things up on their own through trial and error?

In this introduction, I would like to address all these thoughts, as well as a few others, that may come to your mind as you make that first leap into the ranks of management.

First, let me start with a few words on my corporate journey, and how I became the author of this book. I began my life in corporations more than 30 years ago, embarking on what has turned out to be a two-part career: first as a corporate executive and then as a leadership consultant.

For the first 20-odd years, I worked for various U.S. and European multinationals. I assumed my first role as a manager at the ripe age of 26. In the years ahead, I worked in various disciplines such as engineering, marketing, sales and general management. My last position held was that of Asia-Pacific vice-president of an American high-tech corporation. Then, I decided that it was time for me to venture out on my own and do something that has always been my passion: developing people. That was the start of my second career, and I've been doing it for the last 12 years. In this capacity, I worked with high-potential managers ranging from young 20-somethings to experienced and battle-hardened 50-somethings to do only one thing: enhance their success and effectiveness as leaders in corporations.

Truth be told, I'm having much more fun and satisfaction working with people than running businesses. And this is something that I will talk a little more about later in this book.

So why should you spend your time reading a book on the first-time manager? To answer this question, please sit back and imagine that you are about to embark on a new project of great importance to your company. You are the leader of a team of specialists, many of whom you are meeting for the first time. What's the feeling like?

You'd probably feel a tinge of excitement running down your spine. At the same time, you are gripped with some uncertainty and insecurity too. These are some typical questions that you may have:

- What am I expected to do?
- How will my success be defined?
- What are some challenges that I will face? How can I tackle them successfully?
- Are there some new skills and knowledge that I will need? How do I acquire these?
- What's unique about my new role that I must quickly come to grips with?
- I don't know enough about my co-workers. How should I behave towards them?
- How can I get the most out of my team?
- I'm the boss now. If any of my guys get out of line, how should I crack the whip?
- I'm not that comfortable with my boss. What should I do?
- Will I be successful by focusing on doing my job in the best possible way? Or do I need to network and play politics like some managers I know?
- Are there some pitfalls that I must avoid?
- What will help me become more successful?

What are your chances of success then? Most first-time managers, flushed with the idea of becoming a boss for the first time in their career, will think the odds are in their favour.

Having worked with thousands of such managers in various organizations around the world, my observation is that making this transition from an individual contributor to a manager is fraught with difficulties. Nearly all struggle with the new challenges ahead. They soon face a stark reality. They are pretty much on their own and there is no honeymoon period, so to speak. Their superiors expect them to prove their worth from the word "Go". And, by the way, please don't expect much help from bosses. They are under pressure as well and simply too busy to provide guidance to their rookie managers.

However, first-time managers are a hardy and resilient lot. With some help, the majority will make it. Unfortunately, for some people, the experience will be an unpleasant one. Sadly, some will soon decide that being a manager is not their thing. Perhaps, they really don't have what it takes to become managers, they and their bosses will quickly conclude. It is better for them to revert to their previous level and be a specialist or individual contributor. Or does it really have to be this way?

WHAT YOU WILL GET FROM THIS BOOK

Many years ago, I came across a charmingly facetious book about organizational life written by a Canadian educational psychologist, Laurence Peter. It is called *The Peter Principle*.

> *"In any organization, people tend to rise to their level of incompetence."*
> — The Peter Principle

This maxim has intrigued me for many decades since then. I have seen many bright, young and promising people getting themselves trapped by *The Peter Principle* and never achieving their potential as managers and leaders. Yet, I have also worked with countless managers who are better prepared mentally and emotionally for the journey. The speed bumps are still there. There will be tough challenges. But they are much better equipped to handle them. Many of these people not only excel as first-time managers but proceed to move up the next few levels, adding immense value to their organizations and the people with whom they work.

You don't have to fear *The Peter Principle*. It can be circumvented and I'll show you how.

I would like to graphically illustrate the value of this book to first-time managers by using the imagery of a novice explorer venturing into the wilderness. These are what you will get:

1. A map and compass for your journey.
2. A set of useful tools that will help you overcome obstacles along the way. These tools will enable you to make improvisations according to the situations at your workplace.
3. An experienced tour guide who shares lessons learnt from other travellers before you so that you can avoid pitfalls and hidden traps. These will be shared through **managerial anecdotes** sprinkled through the various chapters. Though most of these situations are real, some background details have been modified and pseudonyms are used.
4. A telescope. Why? With the above you're all set for the here and now. A telescope helps you to peek a little beyond your immediate destination, and prepare you for the next steps in your career.

MANAGING THE ASIAN WAY

I would further add that this book is written for managing in an Asian environment. It is meant for Asian managers and their Western counterparts who will work alongside each other in Asia. With China and India fast becoming economic powerhouses, more and more investments are heading towards Asia. Increasingly there will be more Asian managers reaching the upper rungs of management. At the same time, Western managers, especially the younger ones, will want to be stationed in Asia, not just for short-term assignments, but for the long haul.

These self-confident, rising Asian managers and the curious, young Western managers know that it is no longer tenable to apply Western management practices without adaptation. There is visible pride in things Chinese and Indian. This book will therefore blend the best of Western thinking and Eastern wisdom.

WHO WOULD BENEFIT FROM THIS BOOK

This book will be most helpful for the thousands of young people promoted into managerial responsibilities for the first time each year.

Experienced and more senior managers who are facing challenges in leading and managing may find the topics a useful refresher, as they will offer new insights on managing and leading. There is a truism about managing that is worth reminding ourselves about. As we move upwards and acquire even more responsibilities, the basics do not change or become less relevant. True, we'll need to adapt our management styles to more complex situations. Also true is the fact that we'll also need to constantly reinvent ourselves and broaden our repertoire. But we must never lose sight of the basics.

Well-meaning bosses of first-time managers, who are increasingly aware of their pivotal role in helping their new managers succeed, will find this a useful resource. I have also included in the appendices practical information and insights for learning and development practitioners, consultants, academics and executive coaches, who are involved in setting up and delivering leadership development programmes for high-potential employees.

HOW TO GET THE MOST OUT OF THIS BOOK

The first-time manager is a very busy person with many things on her mind, conflicting priorities and insufficient time to get all these accomplished. In writing this book, I have adopted a straightforward, pragmatic and conversational approach. The reading experience is very much like you, the reader, and I are engaged in a friendly and candid chat one topic at a time.

Please note that throughout this book, I will use the pronouns "he" and "she" interchangeably. In my experience, men and women can be equally effective as managers. In fact, I think organizational effectiveness will be further enhanced if more women move up the hierarchy. Various studies in the United States and Europe such as those by McKinsey and Catalyst have shown that companies with the highest proportion of female directors are more profitable and efficient, on the average, than those with the lowest.[1]

You will find 26 brief and easy-to-read chapters that will contain practical ideas that you will need to know and act on. Browse through the book very quickly the first time round to get a feel of what is in store for you. Then come back again and again one chapter at a time. Highlight the pages. Dog-ear them. Write margin notes. Keep a notebook handy so that you can jot down ideas that you find useful.

At the end of each chapter, are the **Anchors** and **Deep Dive** segments, identified by corresponding icons. Anchors are a summary of key takeaways. Deep Dive poses provocative questions for you to reflect on. More importantly, act on them at the workplace.

To conclude this introduction, I'd like to share a Chinese saying.

> *"Learning without thinking is labour lost;*
> *thought without learning is perilous."*
> — Confucius

Let's go one step further by reminding ourselves,

> *"Action without knowledge is irresponsible;*
> *Knowledge without action is a waste of time."*

I welcome feedback from readers. Please email me at bh@leadassociates.com.sg. You can also visit our website at www.leadassociates.com.sg.

My hope is that this book will in some small way facilitate the development of new managers who will spearhead Asia's growth in the 21st century.

Thank you.

—BH Tan

PART ONE

Your Biggest Changes When You Become A Manager

2. Managing Team Members	3. Managing Teams
1. Managing Yourself	
4. Managing Key Relationships	5. Becoming A More Complete Leader

"The journey of a thousand miles
Begins with a single step."
—Tao Te Ching

1 ARE YOU READY TO PLAY A BIGGER GAME?

SUDDENLY, IT IS A MUCH BIGGER WORLD OUT THERE

At workshops for first-time managers, I usually start by saying, "What has got you here will not get you there." This is a line borrowed from Marshall Goldsmith, one of America's pre-eminent executive coaches.

Participants' interest is piqued. And an air of anticipation is created. They wait for me to explain a little more. The most effective way for me to drive home my point is to use a soccer analogy.

Imagine yourself as a skilful and well-regarded member of a soccer team. You have excelled in playing in one of the positions in the team, say, that of a striker or a goalkeeper. You have also been a great teammate, working well with the other players to help your team succeed in various matches. Recently, the coach tapped you to be the new captain of the team. Next week, you will be leading your team into an important match for the first time as the skipper.

Overnight, your view of soccer is transformed!

As an individual player, you are expected to be very competent in playing in a particular position in the team. That means apart from possessing a natural flair, you need a keen interest and a good attitude. You also need to be in the pink of physical condition, and attend a series of training and practice sessions with your team mates. All these enhance the domain expertise that makes you a very good specialist.

During the game, your biggest contribution is to leverage your domain expertise and collaborate with other specialists to score against the opposing team. What you do and how you behave will be in accordance with a pre-set game plan. On the pitch, you will look to one particular player for guidance and inspiration. He is the team captain.

When you become the captain, you play multiple roles. First and foremost, you are the leader of the team, on and off the field. You must command the respect of your players and the trust of the coaches and managers. You will pick your prospective players for their individual skills. Then you must bring them all together and turn them into a high-performing team. You play a key role in defining the game strategy and team formation for every match.

At practice and workout sessions, you need to be a role model. You are the first one on the field and the last one out. You make sure that every player sticks to the workout plan and prescribed diet. What if players don't turn up on time, become disinterested or get out of shape? It's your job to talk to them and to bring them back in line. This is not easy, especially if these people are your buddies.

During the game, you need to be in constant communication with your players so that they are always moving in the direction that was agreed on during practice sessions. Yet you cannot be shouting and yelling all the time.

The situation is very fluid, changing by the moment, as the players on both sides pit themselves against each other. As the skipper, your team triumphs if you have engendered a sense of purpose, esprit de corps, nimbleness in thinking and bold execution. Players read the situation intelligently, seize the opportunities swiftly and perform their own magic while working in synergy with one another. Such a team shines because they work in an environment that nurtures entrepreneurship. The result is improvisation on the spur of the moment, creativity and innovation.

Essentially, you wear two hats. Not only are you the captain, you are a player as well. A good captain might not be the best player in the team. Being the captain, you may, however, be tempted to prove to your fellow players that you are the best by competing with them for the ball. A key question for you will be: What defines my success as a captain? Personally delivering the goals, or orchestrating the team's success by bringing out the genius in all my players?

GOING UP THE VALUE CHAIN

By this, I'm not just referring to the bigger pay packet that you can expect. That will come of course. In return for the bigger bucks that you're getting, the most important difference when you start managing a team is that you are expected to add greater value to your organization compared to what you did previously as an individual contributor.

This is an extremely important point that you must understand and acknowledge. Otherwise, when you get promoted, you will continue doing what you were doing in your previous role because that has become your comfort zone and you were so good at it. Let's now look at a real-life case of a person who failed to go up the value-chain when she became a manager.

Managerial Anecdote

Janet worked for three years as a product specialist in a major healthcare company in Singapore. She learned quickly, and very soon was able to handle very independently the promotional and marketing responsibilities for two hair care products assigned to her. When the marketing manager who was her boss was promoted to lead a larger brand, Janet was the natural successor.

Janet was very pleased to be recognized for her achievements. This promotion would give her a pay raise which would come in handy as she was planning to get married. It was also a first step into management which meant more authority and influence.

As a marketing manager with three product specialists, Janet found her responsibilities expanding significantly. Apart from hair care products she now had skin care in her portfolio. This was very new to her. Of the three product specialists she had to oversee, two were formerly her peers working in skin care. The third one was a new recruit she had taken in for hair care.

Janet found her workday now packed with meetings and presentations. There were many parties she had to meet. Apart from her general manager as well as senior executives from the head office in London, she had to interact with key accounts and vendors. Major product launches were in the works. As she was unfamiliar with the skin care range, she left it entirely to the two product specialists responsible. Her efforts were all devoted to marketing hair care products. Besides, she reasoned, the recruit was too new and inexperienced.

The first six months thus whisked by like a blur. The new product specialist quit after four months in frustration as he felt Janet did not trust him and was micromanaging him every inch of the way. The two other product specialists became very demotivated as Janet had shown very little interest in the skin care products.

A number of product launches were botched. The pressure on Janet mounted, and she left the company a short while later, convinced that she was not cut out to be a manager. She subsequently became a school teacher.

What brought about this rather sad turn of events for Janet? These were some key contributing factors:

- Janet did not have a clue about what was expected of her as a manager compared to her previous role. Neither was she equipped to make the necessary shifts mentally and emotionally.
- She stepped into her new role during a very busy period when new products were being launched. There was literally no time to catch her breath and ask, "What am I supposed to do now?"
- As she was under considerable pressure to deliver results, she quickly defaulted into doing what she was good at in her previous role, i.e. managing hair care, while conveniently leaving what she was unfamiliar with—skin care products—to her two subordinates.
- She did not communicate with her team members, resulting in a lack of common purpose, direction and motivation.
- Her boss, the general manager, did not coach her or help her to settle in and find her footing. In fact, she was thrown into the deep end of the pool by her company.

In a nutshell, Janet did not make a successful transition into her first managerial role.

CRITICAL SHIFTS FOR SUCCESSFUL TRANSITION

When people become managers for the first time, they are in effect undergoing a rite of passage. Like adventurers, they are about to enter a dark and deep mysterious cave. In both Eastern and Western mythologies, we all know that there are fearsome creatures guarding the various thresholds. Those who are unworthy get eliminated quickly. Only the fittest gain safe passage as they slay one dragon after another. At the end of the journey, our heroes emerge stronger, wiser and more resilient.

Professor Linda Hill[1] of Harvard Business School puts it this way, "The first managerial assignment is a pivotal developmental experience for future executives. It is when an executive's basic philosophy and leadership style is shaped....". She then goes on to stress that a "profound adjustment" is required—a transformation of professional identity, no less.

Lessons learnt and experiences gained have shown that the transitional journey to managerial responsibilities involves critical shifts in four areas:

1. Key responsibilities
As a manager your role will become broader and more complex. You are now responsible for your team and not just yourself. A major paradigm shift here for you is the realization that your success now depends on your subordinates. You will succeed only if they succeed. In the same vein, if they are weak and ineffective, you will fail.

"I don't believe this," I hear you protesting. "You mean to say that when I become boss, I become vulnerable because my success is no longer determined by me?" And you had thought that as a manager, you would have full power and authority over your people.

When the truth finally sinks in, some first-time managers default into micromanaging and doing their subordinates' jobs as they do not want to be held ransom by weak subordinates. This is not sustainable and will poison the working atmosphere as Janet had found out. Besides, by doing their subordinates' work they aren't doing what they ought to be doing as a manager.

To ensure success in your new role, you have to create conditions that will help enable your people to succeed. This means understanding what your bosses expect and translating them into results by working through your team members, and coordinating with peers and other functions. And very importantly, to help your people succeed so that you may succeed, you need to coach and develop them.

2. Key skills
Your skills in your previous role as a specialist are useful but no longer sufficient. They were technical or "hard skills" such as data

analysis, project evaluation, trouble-shooting, preparation of a financial report, etc.

At this stage in your career as a first-time manager, you will need to continue acquiring other hard skills such as budgeting, report writing, etc. More importantly, you will need to quickly pick up "soft skills" such as delegating, influencing, communicating, motivating.

Why? Because as a manager you will have to get things done through others. To be able to do this effectively, you will need relational skills, or soft skills. With such skills you will be better able to connect with others and influence them. This is in fact a key determinant of your success. More on this will be discussed in Chapter 5 on EQ.

3. Key stakeholders

When you move up the corporate ladder, you will have a more complex web of relationships with a broader range of stakeholders. While you may have your own team, it isn't sufficient to help you accomplish your goals. You will need to "borrow" other teams' resources. In turn, they will want to leverage on yours as well. So independence needs to co-exist with interdependence. Also noteworthy is the fact that you and these stakeholders may frequently not see eye-to-eye. Your priorities will be different, and your goals may be in conflict.

4. Adding values appropriate to your level[2]

What values are you required to bring to the organization as a manager? How do you know you have added the values that are appropriate to the level that you are in?

In my experience working with managers at all levels, I frequently find this concept largely unrecognized and poorly understood. It is not uncommon even for senior managers to be operating far below their assigned levels. When managers aren't clear about what values are appropriate to their level, they usually default to doing their subordinates' jobs. You will find numerous examples of this in the various anecdotes sprinkled throughout this book.

Let's refer now to the case of Janet in the managerial anecdote. Upon her promotion, her responsibilities were to lead her team of three product specialists to oversee two product categories: hair care as well as skin care.

The values appropriate to her level will be as follows: (a) Achieving results through her team, (b) Guiding and developing her people to be more effective and (c) Enabling her people to excel through appropriate processes, systems and communication.

Unfortunately, she fell short of all three values. She did not lead or develop her people and failed to communicate with them. Instead of providing guidance for work to be done, she left them in the lurch and behaved as though she was still a product specialist for hair care, ignoring the other important part of her portfolio— skin care. And eventually, her poor business results did her in.

IMPLICATIONS ON YOUR CAREER PROGRESSION

As a first-time manager, you are also called a first-line manager. This is the first managerial level in an organization and it requires you to supervise people directly. There are many other levels beyond this. Typically, the next level will be a middle manager who supervises first-line managers. After that, it is a division manager. A step higher will be the general manager. Then a VP, and finally, all the way up to the CEO.

As you climb higher up the corporate ladder, your playing field will continue to expand. There will be bigger responsibilities and expectations, and the challenges that you will handle will become more complex and strategic.

The bottom line is this: throughout your career, in order to continue your upward trajectory, you will have to constantly reinvent yourself by learning, unlearning and relearning. The good news is that the fundamentals that you inculcate as a first-time manager will form a bedrock foundation for you as you scale greater heights. You will be paid back in spades now and then in future if you master the principles explained here.

Many companies are becoming aware that they can't just promote people to managerial positions. They need to help them make the transition as well. This is especially important for first-line managers because they form the pool from which candidates for other management positions will be drawn in the years to come. When companies encounter chronic leadership difficulties at various levels, these can largely be traced back to that first transition into the roles of first-time managers. As these companies expand, they will find that there aren't sufficient capable internal candidates for higher positions.

In contrast, if rookie managers were properly guided in the first leadership transition, they will be better equipped to lead and positively impact their environment and the people who work with them. With the passage of time, they will also grow in experience and capabilities, and be ready for greater responsibilities. With every step up the ladder, they will add and create better value.

It is necessary to recognize that not everybody has the aptitude to become a manager. There are some who prefer to become subject matter experts. If your interests are in this direction, talk to your boss and HR people and explore the possibility of going up the technical ladder instead of the managerial ladder.

- When you become a manager, doing more of what has worked previously will not do. You will have to reinvent yourself in four critical ways.

- Not everybody has the aptitude to become a manager. There are some who prefer to remain as subject matter experts.

Q1: If you were Janet in the managerial anecdote, what would you have done differently when you got promoted?

Q2: What are the values that you need to add as a manager? Who can help you validate that they are appropriate to your level? See the Leadership Turns Framework in Appendix Four.

2 CHARTING YOUR COURSE

FIVE FOUNDATION STONES

In the introduction, I promised you a map and a compass as you set out on your leadership journey. In this section, let me unfold a map. At this point in our discussion, we'll only talk in broad strokes. Details will come in subsequent chapters.

To be effective as a manager, there are five foundation stones that must be in place. These constitute your map as shown below.

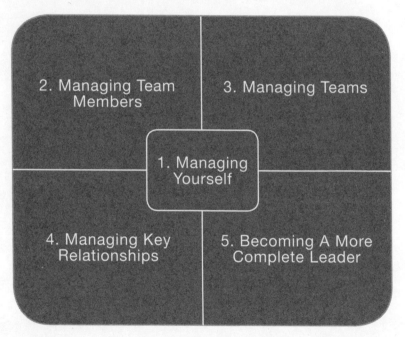

We will work on one foundation stone at a time from Part Two to Part Six of this book. By the time you get to the end of this book, you will have assembled a powerful array of tools suited for different clusters of situations. For greater versatility, it's important for you to improvise as you apply them to different challenges.

KEY SUCCESS INDICATORS (KSIs)

You have just glanced at the map. Can you confidently navigate yourself to your final destination with only a map? Probably not. You will also need a compass that will help set your bearings and, at various checkpoints, give you the assurance that you're on the right track.

What might this compass be? Traditionally, a manager's success is determined by his KPIs or key performance indicators. KPIs invoke quantifiable targets such as sales turnover, productivity improvement or production output. In truth, this is at best a subset of what a manager does. It measures the "what" of managerial work. There is another aspect that is just as important but not accorded the required attention. It is the "how".

There is a saying that in today's organizations, the most valuable assets are mobile. They turn up in the morning and at the end of the day, they walk out of the company's premises. Such knowledge workers have something up their sleeves, so to speak. It is called discretionary effort. They will exercise this discretionary effort and go the extra mile for their employers only when their working environment stimulates them into wanting to do it. Whether such an environment exists can't be neatly defined in quantifiable terms. If it is there, people can feel it. If it is missing, your KPIs stagnate or take a nose-dive.

Hence, to determine a manager's success we need to take into account both the "what" of his accomplishments and the "how" of his leadership style. The concept of Key Success Indicators or KSIs embraces both the "what" and the "how." They may serve as the compass that we are looking for. There will be more in-depth discussion of the importance of balancing the "what" with the "how" in Chapter 4.

Many managers today still go for the "what" as though it is the be-all and end-all. It is quite common to hear organizations being characterized as KPI-driven. Isn't that what managing is all about, these managers might argue. No, more and more enlightened corporations are reminding their managers. They expect managers not only to deliver business results but also lead their people such that they bring out the best in them.

What KSIs will be appropriate to help you navigate on your leadership journey?

Here are some suggestions pertaining to each foundation stone we spoke about earlier.

Managing Yourself
1. You are aware of your strengths and developmental areas.
2. You are making progress in developing yourself.

Managing Team Members
3. There is mutual trust and respect between you and each team member.
4. Through coaching and feedback, you have raised the effectiveness of each team member.

Managing Teams
5. Talented people want to join your team.
6. Your team achieves and even exceeds business goals on a sustainable basis.

Managing Key Relationships
7. You are able to influence others without formal authority.
8. You contribute towards the larger good of your organization.

Becoming a More Complete Leader
9. You lead by example by consciously balancing work and life.
10. You contribute to your community.

MANAGING AND LEADING

In the preceding pages, I have mentioned managing and leading[1], sometimes in the same breath. Do these two words mean the same thing? No, they don't. So what are the differences? As a front-line manager, you will need to be able to do both, though in different proportions. How much of one and how little of the other depends on the situation that you and your team are in.

Managers focus on the present. They provide a sense of purpose and an environment of stability for their people to work together to achieve meaningful and worthwhile objectives. Leaders look into the future. They scan the environment and seek to reposition their teams to be more effective in addressing challenges that are yet to come.

All organizations need both set of capabilities in bosses at every level. Without strong managers, key objectives will not be achieved. Discipline is lacking and there is no sense of urgency. Without strong leaders, the organizations focus only on the short-term. When the future arrives, the organization will be taken off-guard.

As a front-line manager, you will be doing more managing than leading. As a rough guide, I would put the split as 75 percent managing and 25 percent leading. As you move up, the leadership component will increase proportionately.

SUCCESS ENABLERS AND DERAILERS[2]
First-time managers who succeed possess certain behavioural traits or personal characteristics. These are called enablers. There are also certain traits that inhibit success or even cause career failures. These are called derailers. The list that I have compiled in Table 2.1 is based on observations made by myself and other colleagues over many years. It is important to know what these are.

Table 2.1: Success Enablers & Derailers

ENABLERS	DERAILERS
• Deliver results consistently all the time	• Unable to meet business objectives
• Work well with people	• Poor interpersonal skills
• Collaborative; able to give and take	• Silo mindset
• Curious and open-minded	• Unable to learn and adapt
• Politically savvy	• Unreliable/untrustworthy
• Build network and alliances	• Talented people do not want to work with them
• Coach and develop people	• Difficulty managing upwards, sideway and downwards
• Able to influence without formal authority	• Wait for instructions before acting
• Proactive; always one step ahead	
• Lead and impact others positively	
• Communicate clearly and effectively	

• There are five foundation stones which constitute the map for your leadership journey.

• Key Success Indicators (KSIs) take into account both the "what" and the "how" of managerial work.

Q1: Review the matrix on enablers and derailers. Assess yourself. What are your enablers? Do you have potential derailers?

Q2: In your daily work, what is the proportion between managing and leading?

PART TWO
Managing Yourself

2. Managing Team Members	3. Managing Teams
4. Managing Key Relationships	5. Becoming A More Complete Leader

1. Managing Yourself

*"There is nothing noble in being superior to other men.
The true nobility is being superior to your previous self."*
—Hindu proverb

3 DO YOU REALLY KNOW YOURSELF?

HOW MANY VERSIONS ARE THERE OF US?

Through the ages, thinkers in both the East and the West have recognized self-knowledge as the crucial starting point in our journey through life. The following are what two of the greatest philosophers from the East and West have to say about this topic. They both lived nearly three thousand years ago.

> *"Our first and most important priority is self-cultivation*
> *so that we can be the best possible version of ourselves. ...*
> *To know our faults and be able to change is our greatest virtue."*
> —Confucius[1]

> *"Know thyself."*
> —Socrates

It is really worthwhile to pause a while and ask ourselves whether this is really such a big deal. Is it so difficult to know ourselves?

Some years ago in a leadership workshop I was conducting in Seoul for a company, an R&D director in the audience raised his hand and said with thinly veiled impatience, "You say we need to know ourselves so that we can identify what we are good at and what we need to improve on. I agree with this completely. But isn't this a moot point? Who knows us better than we ourselves?"

Strange as it may sound, we are quite complex as human beings and much of our self-discovery is still work in progress. In the course of our daily life and work, we all play different roles. For instance, we are subordinates to our bosses, peers to our colleagues, and boss to the people whom we supervise. It is also like that at home and in other groupings outside work. In each of these settings, we show different facets of ourselves because the context is different. So people experience us differently. Do we then know which of these versions most truly represent us?

A GLIMPSE INTO THE DIFFERENT VERSIONS OF US

So how many versions are there of you? And which version is the real you? Must all the versions be consistent with each other? Let's examine this more closely in the following managerial anecdote.

Managerial Anecdote

Jason worked in one of Taiwan's most prestigious high-tech companies located in the Hsinchu Science Park. As he was considered a "young tiger" in his company, he was put on the fast-track, making him the youngest section manager at the age of twenty-five. Things were going well. He had stepped into his higher responsibilities seemingly without missing a beat. He and this team of engineers were meeting and even exceeding all their targets every month.

Huang was Jason's former boss. Upon Jason's promotion, Huang himself moved upwards and became a department head in another division. Both persons had always got along very well. In fact, Jason considered Huang his mentor.

Six months after Jason became a section manager, Huang invited him for lunch. This was the first time they were meeting since both got promoted. Previously when they were working together, they would have lunch once every two months to touch base. Jason was delighted to meet his former mentor again.

Although Huang was now in a new division, he had established a very trusting and open relationship with people he worked with, both current and former colleagues. Co-workers generally felt comfortable approaching him and seeking his advice. Of late, Huang had heard certain things about Jason as a new manager that he felt Jason ought to be aware of.

Overall, while Jason was indeed managing the business side of his role very well, he had been less successful in his relationship management with his colleagues at various levels. His engineers had begun to see Jason as a know-it-all as he always seemed to have a solution for everything in their meetings. His peers viewed him as rather distant as he had not joined them for any informal gatherings after work. Most senior managers saw Jason very positively as he had done very well so far. However, there were some who felt that he was not contributing much in management meetings when topics outside his immediate responsibilities were tabled.

Jason listened quietly and took all of it in. Huang who knew him very well could sense that beneath the calm demeanour, his former protégé was troubled. He had no idea his co-workers were now experiencing him so differently.

When lunch ended, Jason thanked Huang profusely for the feedback. He knew he had to make some fundamental changes in his relationship with people if he wanted to regain their goodwill and support.

Jason was a fortunate "young tiger" who had someone older looking out for him. He had not the slightest clue what people were saying about him until he had lunch with Huang. One would have thought that at the very least, his immediate boss would have provided him some feedback. That, of course, did not happen. Unfortunately, receiving little or no feedback is a common phenomenon in organizations, not just in Asia, but Europe and the United States.

There were various reasons for the lack of feedback for Jason. For one, Jason was doing extremely well so far in meeting his numbers. In most organizations, numbers is king. If you hit all of them month after month, you're golden and people at all levels see you as a star. The corporate culture could also be another major factor. Perhaps, providing feedback simply was not a common practice.

IMPORTANCE OF SELF-AWARENESS

What would the consequences be if Jason had continued to exhibit, albeit unwittingly, the behaviours to subordinates, peers and bosses that Huang had described?

The short answer to this is that it wouldn't be long before he would run into a road block. His subordinates would clam up in his presence. Peers might start to isolate him as his behaviours were getting stand-offish. And when the numbers that were keeping him safe so far started to slip, bosses would quickly point out a number of things that Jason wasn't doing right all this while.

Going back to what Confucius said at the opening of this chapter, Jason would have failed to show the best possible version of himself.

DIFFERENT EXPECTATIONS AND RESPONSIBILITIES

As you become a first-time manager, a major realization to grasp is that unlike in your previous role as a specialist, there are now different expectations of you from the different constituencies. And your role is much more complex.

Broadly, your responsibilities are planning, communicating, managing your team and coordinating with other functions to ensure that business objectives are met. The three main constituencies will have different expectations as follows:

- **Subordinates:** They would like you to provide clear definitions of what the company expects while guiding, motivating and developing them.
- **Peers:** They prefer you to communicate openly and collaborate with them.
- **Bosses:** They will look forward to you delivering as per their expectations, keeping them posted and actively engaging with them.

Apart from these three constituencies, you may have to consider others such as customers and vendors as well. It becomes quickly clear that there are some inherent conflicts in all these expectations, and reconciling them becomes a necessary skill. And this is key. For instance, bosses will expect you to get more out of your subordinates, while your subordinates expect you to stand up for them.

The image you project as a manager will be defined by your success in balancing the conflicting needs of all the constituencies which at times appear to be pulling you in different directions.

HOW CAN YOU ENHANCE SELF-AWARENESS?

There is no short-cut. Start by being humble and realizing that different people around you see you differently. Their views may all have validity. Make it a point of building mutually trusting and helpful relationships with co-workers so that when you occasionally seek input about yourself, they are willing to be open and candid with you.

Before you even approach others, start with some honest introspection. These are some questions you may want to ponder on and write down in your notebook:

1. In three different words, how would I describe myself?
2. What aspects of my work do I like best?
3. What aspects of my work do I like least?
4. What are my two key strengths?
5. What are my two key weaknesses?
6. In three different words, how would my subordinates describe me?
7. In three different words, how would my peers describe me?
8. In three different words, how would my bosses describe me?
9. In three different words, how would I like to be described?
10. What are my three core values?
11. How will my family members describe me?

When you feel that the timing is correct and you have established a sufficiently open and trusting relationship with your co-workers, you may approach them individually for some input. Before you do this, think of an appropriate way of bringing up the topic. Informal is best. Perhaps, after a short meeting with a peer, you may ask her whether she is able to spare a few minutes with you to give you some suggestions for your own self-development. Then ask only one question: "What should I do more of to be more effective in my work?"

Listen fully. Do not interrupt or defend, even if you do not agree with what they are saying. Thank them. And when you are alone, reflect on the input received. When you have heard from many different people, a pattern will emerge in your mind. We will discuss more about this process in Chapter 13.

THE IMPORTANCE OF CORE VALUES

Your core values are the aspects of life that you consider of central importance. They are your key drivers and form part of your identity. You are happiest when you are working in an environment, or involved in activities, that are consistent with your values. Conversely, people find it stressful to have to act contrary to their values.

Examples of values are: integrity, tradition, being genuine, power, security, fairness, fun, etc. Be aware of what your values are. In your work as a leader, be consistent with your values in both your words and deeds. If you are able to do that, you will find satisfaction and inner peace in your career. Otherwise, you will be conflicted and will not come across as authentic. This will not augur well for the long journey ahead.

- To be effective as a leader and a person, the starting point is to have greater self-awareness.

- People will have different perspectives of you because of the different roles that you play.

Q1: Compare and contrast the responses to Q1, Q6, Q7, Q8, Q9 and Q11. What are you learning about yourself? How should you reconcile the differences?

Q2: When you approach others to ask for their perception of you, why should you listen completely and not interrupt or defend, even if you don't agree with what is being said?

4 WHAT KIND OF LEADER DO YOU WISH TO BE?

RESULTS-ORIENTATION AND PEOPLE-ORIENTATION

Nearly all leaders are conflicted by having to choose between results-orientation and people-orientation. Underpinning this is the implicit assumption that the two approaches are mutually exclusive. To put it simply, many people think that if you want to achieve results, you can't be people-oriented. Conversely, if you are a people-oriented person, then get ready to be at best average when it comes to delivering results.

But do these hold true? And are you results-oriented or people-oriented? Is it possible to be both?

Managerial Anecdote 1

Some years ago, the Australian HR Vice President of a huge European technology company invited me to meet up with his American Chief Executive Officer who was on one of his regular visits to Asia. On the day of the appointment, I was ushered into a corner office. Both the CEO and the HR VP were already seated.

Apparently, they had been in discussion for a while before I arrived. After a brief introduction by the HR VP, whom I had known for quite a few years, the CEO explained that he would like me to consider coaching his Thai Operations VP.

The situation was as such: in the last three weeks, during which the company was in the midst of a merger with a larger competitor, three directors in different parts of Asia contacted the HR VP to inform him that they were planning to quit. These directors all worked for the Operations VP. The reason each offered was similar: they could no longer stomach the command-and-control leadership style of their boss. Not only were they constantly micromanaged, they felt undermined and put down by the Operations VP's abrasive and "what have you done for me lately?" attitude.

When the CEO heard about this, he was naturally alarmed and decided to make an urgent trip to Asia to carry out a series of skip-level meetings with the three directors and others. The CEO then referred to his notes and shared some verbatim remarks that he had received such as: "All he cared about were results, results and results. Nothing else mattered", "There was no room to offer differing opinions. It was his way or the high way" and "I'm perfectly able to lead my people to achieve or even exceed our KPIs. But he has to interfere in every which way".

The CEO paused, put his notes aside and wearily continued, "He is our best performing operations VP across the regions. None of his counterparts in North America, Latin America and Europe can hold a candle to the business results he has achieved. But admittedly, I have always known that he can be rough with his people."

I very much wanted to raise an obvious question. But he answered it himself, "Each year, at his annual performance review, I would ask him to be more considerate to his people... Now I realize that there isn't much teeth to what I've been telling him. As long as the goods are being delivered in his region, I pretty much leave him alone.

I guessed I have allowed business performance to override everything for far too long. His senior people are up in arms and are threatening to bail out now unless I remove this tyrant from the region!"

This is a classic case that is played out every day in various organizations around the world. Results often take top precedence and if you do well here, bosses are willing to turn a blind eye to your "rough" side, as this CEO had put it. Countless managers have in fact climbed rapidly up the career ladder by delivering on their numbers at all cost, including riding roughshod over all who were standing in their way. Sadly, many bosses and companies are willing to put up with this kind of behaviour as they don't want to kill the goose that lays the golden egg. However, the day of reckoning will come, as is evident in this case when the CEO's hand was forced.

This episode did not have a happy ending. Two months later, when the merger was consummated, the CEO, as well as his Asian Operations VP, found themselves without a job.

Managerial Anecdote 2

In a recent performance appraisal review, Audrey was delighted to know that her boss had rated her as outstanding for the work that she had done in the last nine months as a newly promoted manager. She was deemed to be very effective in leading her team and accomplishing all the objectives agreed.

One remark from her boss troubled her though. She couldn't quite figure out what he was driving at when he said, "Being people-oriented is fine. But do remember that what matters here is your ability to achieve your KPIs." What was he trying to tell me, she kept asking herself. Am I too soft with my people?

How would you interpret what Audrey's boss said to her? How would you react if you were in her shoes?

Audrey was one of the many first-time managers whom I have worked with. The upshot of what her boss said to her was that she became intentionally less accessible to her team. Where there used to be an atmosphere of camaraderie and friendly banter, a more cut and dried approach emerged—less discussion and more "just do as you are told."

Audrey, who was by nature an outgoing and bubbly person, was soon feeling, in her own words, "like a jerk". She could sense that her people were also drifting away from her.

She decided to call me out for a chat one day. After hearing about her predicament, I reminded her about the principle of Yin and Yang. You will find out more about this concept later in this chapter.

She became silent for a long time. Then she chided herself, "Why wasn't I mindful of that? Yes, we did discuss that at length before. All that it took to knock me off my balance was one pointed remark from my boss."

In the weeks ahead, Audrey regained her groove. She continued delivering her numbers while remaining respectful and approachable to her people.

"EITHER-OR" VERSUS "BOTH-AND"

The mental block that managers around the world are battling against may be said to be caused by the "either-or" mentality.

I would like to share a vivid example of this kind of thinking. Twenty years ago, the president of the consumer products division of AT&T was visiting Asia. His company was then the market leader in cordless phones in the United States. As he toured Hong Kong, Taiwan, China and South Korea, he noticed that numerous Asian upstarts were introducing low-cost versions of cordless phones. But he wasn't impressed as he could see that they generally looked and felt tacky. The sound was far from the "crystal clear" quality that his brand promised. Besides, these cheap brands did not have the cachet of AT&T.

Over dinner, he shared his observations with me. My take was that Asian companies were hungry, and like the Japanese before them, they would keep improving their products until one day, they could match the best Western offerings in quality. And at a much lower price to boot. He was incredulous. His riposte: "Cheap things are never good. Good things are never cheap." Today, AT&T is no longer in the consumer products business. The best consumer electronic products are manufactured in Taiwan, China, Japan and Korea.

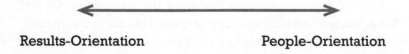

Results-Orientation   **People-Orientation**

Diagram 4.1: Results-orientation/People-orientation Continuum

In Diagram 4.1, results- and people-orientation are arrayed as polar opposites between which there is a huge gulf. It is a binary way of looking at things: 1 or 0. Most people are torn apart by the seemingly irreconcilable differences.

There is another way of looking at the situation. Between results- and people-orientation is not a chasm but a continuum. Why confine ourselves only to the two polar opposites?

This is a self-limiting mindset. Can we not play along the whole spectrum? We may combine results-orientation with people-orientation in different proportions depending on the situations we are facing. In other words, let's reject the tyranny of the "either-or" notion and instead opt for the infinite possibilities of the "both-and" approach.

For instance, when pursuing a difficult deadline, the manager with the "either-or" mindset will drive his people relentlessly and constantly harp on the consequences of not finishing the task on time. On the other hand, the manager with the "both-and" mindset will adopt a more nuanced approach—motivating his team members to meet the deadline while keeping up the team spirit. Which approach will be more effective? No prize for guessing this correctly.

This concept of complementarity has been understood and embraced for centuries in East Asian societies such as China, Korea and Japan. It is traceable to Lao Tzu, an older contemporary of Confucius (551-479 B.C.), and the author of *Tao Te Ching* or *The Book of the Way*. It is also commonly known as Yin Yang.

The Yin Yang symbol consists of a circle divided into two fish-shaped halves—much akin to a black dolphin with a white eye intertwining with a white dolphin with a black eye. These represent the opposing forces or energies found in nature—black/white, positive/negative, male/female, hard/soft, analytical/intuitive and so on.

According to Lao Tzu, harmony in nature comes about through the constant interaction of Yin and Yang forces or energies. Thus what is black will gradually become white and then black again. It is a natural order of things for ebbs and flows to occur like the waves lapping the shore.

Diagram 4.2: Yin Yang symbol

Another important point in this concept is that every polarity contains the seed of its opposite as represented by the white eye in the black dolphin and the black eye in the white dolphin. Thus Yin and Yang cannot be separated but must be considered as whole. As such, there is undeniable wisdom in the saying, "It's not all black or all white."

Hence in the Eastern tradition, thinking is not linear and analytic. It's more circular and holistic, giving rise to a more balanced perspective about work and life challenges.

In contrast, according to Fritjof Capra, the famous Austrian-born American physicist who wrote the best-selling book *The Tao of Physics*, Western culture favours "self-assertion over integration, analysis over synthesis, rational knowledge over intuitive wisdom, science over cooperation, expansion over conservation, and so on. This one-sided development has now reached a highly alarming stage; a crisis of social, ecological, moral and spiritual dimensions."

I frequently wonder where AT&T Consumer Products will be today if its president had set this vision for the company, "A cordless phone in every home with crystal-clear sound quality at an affordable price."

A LEADERSHIP MODEL FOR THE 21ST CENTURY[1]

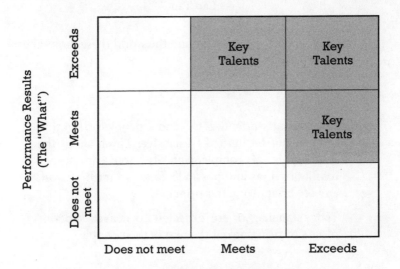

Diagram 4.3: The "what" vs the "how"

The above diagram quite aptly depicts the classic dilemma faced by managers around the world for the longest time—the long-standing struggle between results- and people-orientation. Enlightened companies now define "key talents" as people who are able to do both the "what" and the "how".

By tuning into Lao Tzu's theory, we may discover a way of having the best of both worlds, so to speak. With some imagination, we may envision this sage from ancient China saying this to the netizens of the 21st century:

"Whatever you do, approach it in a measured
and balanced manner. Neither be purely results-oriented nor
completely people-oriented. When a situation goes to its extreme, it
is bound to turn around and be the other.
A good leader is one who delivers superior business results
by bringing out the best in her people."
— Lao Tzu

Many enlightened companies around the world these days expect
no less from their managers.

- Results-orientation and people-orientation need not be mutually exclusive. Think about the principle of complementarity. You can unlock infinite options and possibilities for yourself at work and life by applying this principle.

- Today's managers are expected to deliver superior results by bringing out the best in their people.

Q1: Look around you at the workplace. Do people tend to be more results-oriented or people-oriented? What impact do they have on people around them? What kind of leader is your boss?

Q2: Where do you place yourself now in Diagram 4.3? Where do you wish to be?

5 WHY EQ MATTERS A GREAT DEAL

IQ VS EQ

(emotional intelligence)

Conventional wisdom had it that to succeed in work and life, IQ was the determining factor. Hence, if we had excellent grades in our schools or at the universities, prospective employees would take these as a mark of superior intelligence, that presumably would equate to high achievements at work.

While there is no doubt that IQ is a very important factor, in the last few decades society at large has begun to recognize that there is something else that is an even more powerful predictor of success. We see examples of this every day in our workplaces, our homes and in our communities. For instance, your fast-expanding company recruited a number of fresh graduates a few years ago. Among the recruits, there were a couple of people who had won the highest academic honours in their schools. While the rest were still pretty impressive, they could not match the sterling scholastic records of the top two.

Fast forward two to three years into the future. You would have expected the two brilliant persons to have surpassed their cohorts in climbing up the corporate ladder. But no, the people who had flourished were those with lesser academic credentials. And you were puzzled.

What is at work here? Invariably, this has something to do with a concept called Emotional Intelligence or its casual shorthand EQ.

Let's discuss what EQ is after we look at the following managerial anecdotes.

Managerial Anecdote 1

Yang was interviewing for the post of General Manager with a large manufacturing company located in the south of China. He had already met three senior executives a few weeks ago at the company.

The last three interviews had gone off without a hitch, and he was invited to meet the president of the company. The headhunter who brokered interviews said that this would be the final hurdle, and that the president would make him the offer if all proceeded according to plan.

Yang met the president James Wong at the office. Mr. Wong was warm, friendly and unpretentious. Yang had expected the boss to be somewhat formal and a little pompous. The founder of the company, Mr. Wong, was educated in the United States and had worked in the Silicon Valley for many years. In the late 1970s, as China opened itself to the world, he decided to return to Hong Kong. He was one of the first entrepreneurs to be invited into the special economic zone of Shenzhen.

Yang was pleasantly surprised that the president was so relaxed and personable. It didn't really seem like an interview. After lunch, the president offered to accompany him to the airport to catch his flight. There was a lot of light-hearted conversation along the way. As they reached the airport, the president turned to Yang with a disarming smile and asked cheerily, "Tell me what is the reason I should offer you the position of GM."

Yang swallowed and blanched. This was followed by an awkward silence. Then, he hurriedly opened the door and said, "I'm surprised that you ask me this after so many interviews. I'll leave it to you to decide."

With that, he got out in a huff, leaving his host stunned.

In Anecdote 1, how would you diagnose the sudden turn of events? Obviously, Yang had misjudged the intent of the president's parting question. He had taken offence when none was intended. His host was on the cusp of offering him the job. In his offhanded way, he had posed the question almost rhetorically. All Yang had to do was to respond in an equally light-hearted way. Yet, he interpreted that as yet another probing and searching question meant to assess his worth after many arduous rounds of interview. Basically, Yang kissed the coveted job good-bye with his outburst.

Managerial Anecdote 2

Emily was the employee relationship manager of a large retail chain. Although she was young and had been in this role for only two years, she had already acquired a reputation as someone to go to if employees had any problems at work. It wasn't unusual for employees to make appointments to seek her advice on issues ranging from indifferent supervisors to rude customers. All of them would walk away feeling "lighter", "understood" and "appreciated". These were the three most commonly used words to describe their sessions with Emily.

When Emily was asked by her admiring manager what transpired during her discussions with these employees, she would modestly say, "I'd close the door to my office and devote my full attention to the person sitting in front of me. I listen mostly and encourage her to speak up and assure her of full confidentiality. Sometimes, I do offer some suggestions, but in the majority of cases, these colleagues seem to know what to do when the conversation ends. I do call them to follow up a day or two later. With their permission, I sometimes speak to their bosses to let them know what we have discussed. I usually find that they generally return to their workplace with a greater sense of purpose. If there had been a misunderstanding between them and their bosses, somehow this helps both parties to open up a dialogue. And they are better able to work with each other."

In Anecdote 2, troubled employees kept coming to Emily because she was always approachable and patient. Even managers would send their so-called recalcitrant employees to Emily. Her listening skills were great, and employees sensed her empathy when they were pouring out their sorrows to her. She provided a safe oasis for people to speak to her in confidence. And in that climate, people felt understood. Hence, people usually left with a lighter burden than when they came in. And in the event that she had to circle back to the managers themselves, her input was valued and helped break the impasse that had existed previously.

SO WHAT IS EQ?

Daniel Goleman popularized the concept of EQ with his landmark book *Emotional Intelligence: Why It Can Matter More Than IQ*. EQ consists of five main components.[1]

Component 1: Self-awareness

In Chapter 3, we spent much time on why and how we may know ourselves better. In addition to this, it is very important to be fully present as life unfolds! We seldom pay attention to how we feel. That's because with the fast-paced life that we all lead, we are bombarded constantly by endless streams of data and thoughts. Our moods may therefore vary from moment to moment. Are we anxious, angry, feeling elated or insecure? It isn't sufficient to be experiencing these different moods, we need to be in touch with them. The Buddhists call this "mindfulness". When we are mindful, we are fully attuned to our emotions. Our self-awareness enables us to be consciously in touch with the here and now.

For instance, a senior manager senses that his subordinates tend to defer to him during discussions. In countless meetings, the moment he expresses an opinion, free flow of ideas will cease. In order to encourage his people to speak up, he therefore resolves to be more relaxed and casual in meetings. He makes it a point to listen patiently and invite others to share their opinions. Over a period of time, his subordinates become more comfortable in his presence.

Component 2: Self-Regulation

With mindfulness, we will be in a better position to choose the most appropriate response to the situation at hand. Otherwise, we become completely at the mercy of what is evolving, like the proverbial puppet jerked around by the unseen strings of external events. As the saying goes, "Between a stimulus and response, there is a choice."

Imagine this scenario: when driving to work, another motorist tailgated you for what seemed to be the longest time. Then he suddenly overtook you. Obviously, you became upset. You wanted to give chase and show him your displeasure.

Here, the stimulus was the provocative act by that driver. The instinctive response was to retaliate. But you quickly decided you had other choices. The one you eventually chose was the wiser and saner one. By remaining calm, you reached your office safely and in a positive mood.

Component 3: Motivation

People with high EQ are much better in marshalling their emotions to facilitate achievement of their goals. For instance, you may be conflicted by having to make a difficult decision. Procrastination seems to be a nice way of delaying the pain. You tell yourself nonetheless that further delay will not do and you commit to making up your mind over the weekend.

Component 4: Empathy

This is the flip-side of self-awareness. It is "other awareness" or the ability to sense the emotions in the people around us. When we are communicating with others, they are constantly sending cues to us concerning how we are affecting them. The cues come not only through words, but also through gestures, facial expressions, and tone of voice. In the Asian environment, there is yet another powerful signal: "unspoken words" or silence. Some people can pick these up immediately and quickly make the necessary adjustment in what they are saying to stay connected with their audience. Others, however, may miss them completely and behave inappropriately. A case in point is Yang, the hapless candidate in Managerial Anecdote 1.

Component 5: Social Skill

This is the litmus test of EQ. All of us have sat in at lectures conducted by different speakers. Granted that the topics are all different, how engaged we are is very much determined by the persona of the speaker and the way she behaves on the stage. If she is enthusiastic, energetic and warm, the audience will respond in kind. On the other hand, if we get a speaker who is disinterested and ill-prepared, we can sense it immediately and will tune out. This is the power of emotional connection or rapport building. It is contagious. Leaders with high EQ can leverage their emotional state and send positive ripples of energy through others.

EQ: THE DIFFERENTIATING FACTOR

"EI abilities rather than IQ or technical skills emerge as the discriminating competency that best predicts who among a group of very smart people will lead most ably."
—Daniel Goleman

Earlier, we were puzzled to learn that work performance may not be co-related to high academic grades. Those who excel in companies possess the unique ability of being able to deliver outstanding results through people. They do this through leveraging their high EQ.

This is not to say that IQ is not important. It is. We can view IQ as a threshold quality. If a candidate for a post does not possess certain academic credentials (read IQ) he won't even be selected. When he joins the company with the required credentials, he will find that people around him are generally highly intelligent. In such an environment, the differentiator will be EQ. In other words, a person who possesses both good IQ and EQ will be more successful than someone who relies only on IQ.

Here are some examples of the impact of EQ on workplace performance:
- Programmers in the top 10% of EQ competency develop software three times faster
- High EQ sales people produce twice the revenue of average performers
- In all professions, when high IQ people fail, 75% of the factors are due to poor EQ

How does high EQ manifest itself in the workplace? There are many people who confuse high EQ with being nice, sensitive and not upsetting others.

If you observe people around you, you will notice that there are some individuals who are in touch with how they are feeling at the moment. They are also socially aware of the emotions that others are experiencing and why they are feeling that way. Such people relate well with others because they can put themselves in their shoes. Under stress they remain calm because they can regulate their emotions. Like the proverbial duck in the pond, they may be paddling furiously under the water but they still exude poise and confidence. In tough situations, they don't go out of kilter as they know that such events will pass and they will bounce back. This is resilience.

Though high EQ people are pleasant to work with, there is a tougher edge to them.as well. They do not go out to be nice and get everybody to like them. They will not flinch from speaking the truth because it will upset others. However, they will pick their battles, and find the right place and time to make their point. As a manager, they will uphold high standards of performance and behavior.

CAN EQ BE DEVELOPED?

Since EQ is so crucial to success, what can one do about it? Unlike IQ which is innate, EQ can be enhanced and developed further. You may notice that generally as people grow older, they somehow work better with others. There is an old-fashioned word to describe this. It is called maturity.

But for practical reasons, we all can't sit around and wait for advancing age to enhance our EQ. Besides, we all know of some co-workers who remain just as feisty and insufferable as they enter their old age.

In the next chapter, we'll discuss how you may develop your EQ.

- At work, people generally possess high IQ. However, the quality that differentiates smart people is their EQ level.

- EQ can be developed. It starts with self-awareness and will require practice, practice and more practice.

Q1: Review the managerial anecdotes involving Yang and Emily. What strike you as the key differences in the way they conducted themselves?

Q2: Review the five components that make up EQ. Rate yourself on each component on a scale of 1-10 with 10 being ideal.

6 DEVELOPING YOURSELF

LEARNING, UNLEARNING AND RELEARNING

"The illiterate of the 20th century was a person who could not read or write. The illiterate of the 21st century is a person who can't learn, unlearn and relearn."
— Alvin Toffler

When I think about the countless managers I have come across over the years, a clear and distinguishing trait emerges between those who continue to progress upwards in their career trajectories and those who soon reach their plateau. It is their learning agility.

People who grow from strength to strength are those who are able to learn faster and more effectively. This is not acquisition of more knowledge per se. Picking up an MBA, reading more books or journals, or attending more seminars will not make much of a difference.

People who possess learning agility seem to have a learning strategy, if intuitively. They understand that things need to change when they change roles or positions. And they excel in a lifelong habit of reinventing themselves through "learning, unlearning and relearning."

Let's pause awhile and consider. Why should we unlearn? Isn't all past learning useful? If so, aren't we better off learning, learning and learning? In other words, let's simply pile it high, wide and deep.

Let's review a case that speaks about this.

Managerial Anecdote
Li Wen had worked for three years as a sales representative. She had performed very well, consistently exceeding her quotas year over year. Her boss was very impressed not only by her flair for closing deals but

also by the good relationship she had cultivated with her customers. The following year, Li Wen was promoted to sales manager overseeing five other sales representatives.

As a sales manager, her responsibility was to guide her team to meet the company's sales objectives for the region that she was in charge of. She was no longer required to personally bring in the sales herself.

Talking about learning, unlearning and relearning, if you were Li Wen, what do you need to do to reinvent yourself for your new role?

Li Wen is great at sales and managing relationships with her customers. As a manager, this track record that she possesses is invaluable. Her team members will definitely view her with great respect. But she cannot continue to rely on her personal selling skills as a manager. Her new responsibilities will include planning, budgeting, strategizing and sales force management. These are areas that are new to her and she will have to learn all these quickly.

What does she need to unlearn? A consummate sales person such as Li Wen loves the adrenalin rush in closing big accounts. She also delights in establishing customer intimacy. Yet, she now knows it is not the proper use of her time to continue closing deals personally. That is not her job. What she needs to do more of is to set objectives for her people and then help them to close deals. She must now get her adrenalin rush from knowing that when her people are successful, she becomes successful.

I hear you asking, "Won't it be a monumental waste of talent if she now tries to "unlearn" these skills that have underpinned her success?" Absolutely. However, that will be a misinterpretation of the notion of unlearning. Nobody is saying that she must now bury these unique skills. She can continue leveraging them albeit in different ways.

For instance, she can coach her sales representatives in the art of selling, closing deals and relationship building. This is in fact a key requirement of her job. By doing this well, she will multiply herself, so to speak. Imagine how much more successful her team will be if Li Wen is gradually able to raise the capability of each sales representative.

Another way she can muster her talents will be to occasionally provide "artillery support" for her people when they need to interact with the big guns, or more influential decision-makers, from the clients' side.

Her skills will also come in handy within her own company when she needs to interact with senior management. Selling her ideas and thoughts to the big brass in the company is an important aspect of her managerial role.

Since this is now only her first year as a manager, there will be plenty of opportunities for her to relearn what she might have learnt previously. Let's explore this a little more.

Have you experienced re-reading a book after a lapse of a few years? Sometimes, to our surprise, we find new and deeper meaning in the passages. Why? Possibly because certain events might have happened in the intervening period that occasioned some soul-searching. The words that we chance upon in that book merely flesh out the lessons that lie beneath the surface.

And so it will be for Li Wen. As a new manager, she will experience many successes and set-backs. Hopefully, these will lead her to re-examine assumptions and concepts that she has held as sacrosanct. The relearning will lead to greater maturity of thoughts and resilience of character.

HARD SKILLS AND SOFT SKILLS

As a first-time manager, you will need more of two kinds of skills: hard skills and soft skills.

Hard skills are technical skills such as budgeting, financial management, problem-solving and decision-making, forecasting, report writing, etc. What exactly these are will depend on the role that you playing. Talk to your boss and ask him for his advice.

If need be, request for your company to send you for training to equip you with these skills.

You will also need soft skills. These are people skills. Some examples of soft skills are: presentation skills, negotiation, conflict resolution, delegation, coaching, etc. Many companies do have training programmes for these as well. As you settle into your new role, you will get a better sense of what training programmes will benefit you. Discuss with your boss and your learning organization or training coordinators about these as well.

Many, if not all, the people skills that you need will be EQ related. The rest of this book will be about people skills.

✳ A MODEL FOR DEVELOPING YOURSELF

The first step to developing yourself is to be more self-aware. This was covered in Chapter 3. Find a quiet weekend and be by yourself without the distraction of friends and family members. Working through findings from your introspection and feedback from others, ask yourself what two behaviours you will need to focus on improving or developing so that you can connect better with others.

To answer this question, you will need to look back at recent incidents as well as other critical events in your life. There is no need to hurry here. Pause and reflect. Slowly but surely, you will discern a pattern in your style of interaction.

Some typical examples that arise are:

- I know I'm impatient and impulsive. This has led to a lot of ill-conceived decisions that I later regret.
- I don't listen well and tend to interrupt people.
- My people are intimidated by me because I am so serious and unsmiling.
- I'm too nice. People take advantage of me because I can't say "No".

Be realistic. Start with one, or at most, two behaviours. Ask what you will do differently. For instance, to improve on your listening ability, you may decide on taking three actions:

1. Show patience and attentiveness when others are speaking;
2. Refrain from interrupting others; and
3. Show genuine interest in others' opinions.

These actions will form the basis of your Personal Development Plan (PDP). Try completing Table 6.1 on page 65 yourself. Your next step will be to implement your PDP. Self-development requires hard work and dedication. Improving one's EQ is not an intellectual exercise. It involves a shift in one's behaviours and will not occur overnight. It will take months and sometimes even years.

THE EXPERIENTIAL LEARNING MODEL[1]

Here is a four-step model that can serve as a guide for your self-development. We will use "improving listening ability" as an example.

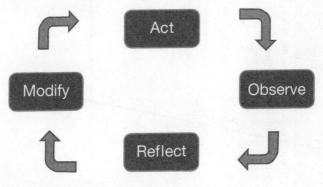

Diagram 6.1: The Experiential Learning Model

Step 1: **Act.** When you interact with your co-workers, consciously apply 1, 2 and 3.

Step 2: **Observe.** Be aware of how others are responding to your actions.

Step 3: **Reflect.** When you find some quiet time, ask yourself, "How did they react to me? What have I done well? What should I modify?"

DEVELOPMENT AREAS	ACTIONS	TARGET DATES	KEY SUCCESS INDICATORS
SAMPLE To become a better listener	1. When others come into my office, I will devote complete attention to them. 2. Refrain from interrupting when others are speaking. 3. Stay relaxed and show genuine interest.	xxxx	1. My co-workers feel that their opinions matter to me. 2. Mutual trust is enhanced. 3. Important issues are raised and resolved, resulting in greater teamwork and productivity.
1.			
2.			

Table 6.1: Personal Development Plan (PDP)

Step 4: Modify. This means making some improvements arising from Step 3 and repeating Step 1.

They key to successful application of the Experiential Learning Model lies in learning from what you have done. While experience is the best source of learning, not everybody learns from experience.[2] Partner with a peer whom you trust and discuss your experience. This is peer coaching. In Chapters 10 and 11 you will learn more about coaching. Having someone to talk with will facilitate your learning. Over many months, your new behaviour will gradually become second nature to you. People around you will notice the change and start responding positively to you.

PLAY TO YOUR STRENGTHS

It is important to note that you will be much more successful if you "play to your strengths." Simply put, in all of us, there are a few things that we do very well in because they come naturally to us. You might say we were born with such a flair. Or past experiences might have given us such an edge. An example of a strength may be our ability to present clearly, confidently and convincingly.

Sure, there are areas we need to develop further. For instance, our grasp of financial management concepts may be inadequate. Hence, when we make a presentation to senior management, we will do a great job until we come to the financial part. That's when we get a little shaky and uncomfortable.

So what do we do? It all depends on whether that inadequacy is a fatal flaw. A fatal flaw has to be fixed, no question about it. An abrasive style towards your co-workers, for instance, will be a fatal flaw. If you do not make real and lasting change in the way you behave towards others, your career will likely derail.

In other cases, the weakness may not be fatal. Returning to the presentation example, let's say you are an R&D manager presenting a project proposal to a panel of senior managers. You have a good way of speaking and are very credible in the eyes of these bosses. Your biggest bugbear, however, is the financial part of the presentation. You're just not good with financial data.

What can you do about this? In the past, you tried to bone up on the numbers portion. However, it didn't help. In fact, you became rather edgy and nervous throughout the presentation, adversely affecting your overall delivery. You were effectively playing to your weakness.

So what else can you do to circumvent this weakness? One possible approach to consider is to ask one of your team members who's financially savvy to partner you in the presentation. You will do the overall part while he'll do the number portions. This is one instance in which you play to your strengths.

- As a first-time manager, hard skills are still important. Continue acquiring them with the help of your boss and the learning organization.

- People skills will be vital for your success. They are all EQ related. Understand and adopt the Experiential Learning Model.

Q1: What are your two key strengths?

Q2: What two leadership behaviours would you need to develop further? How will you implement your PDP?

7 TIME MANAGEMENT

WORKING HARD BUT NOT WORKING SMART

A common challenge that managers will encounter is that each day they are faced with an endless stream of work coming in while time is constantly in short supply. As a result, working hours become extended. Many will respond by staying very late at the office or taking work home.

There is much good to be said about developing a strong work ethic of being dedicated and diligent, and doing whatever it takes to get the job done. However, if long hours become a norm rather than an exception, it may not be about work ethics. It may be a common case of working hard but not working smart.

Let's consider the situation that Raja, a newly minted manager, is experiencing three months into his new role.

Managerial Anecdote

As Raja sips his latte at his favourite neighbourhood café on a balmy Saturday morning, he is deep in thought. So much has changed in such a short time, he muses. Three months ago, he was a happy-go-lucky production planner. Now he is the boss, as his friends are calling him. "Boss" refers to the position of production planning manager with a team of experts working for him.

He has to stifle a woeful smile that is curling up his lips. If only I had known that being boss means so much more paperwork, endless meetings, making unpopular decisions and answering for so many things that I do not directly control, he mutters to himself.

It's time to get a grip, he scolds himself. Let me list down my key activities on a typical day. Perhaps with that, I'll be able to figure out how I should organize my workday differently. With that idea in mind, he switches on his laptop and types in the following points.

1. *My day starts with a bang: (a) urgent phone calls, (b) incoming emails, or (c) people walking into my office. Approximately 2 hours*
2. *Attends two to three meetings lasting 1 hour to 1.5 hours each. Total time spent: 3.5 hours*
3. *Bosses suddenly summon me for a quick chat: 1 hour*
4. *Peers coming in to talk on work: 1 hour*
5. *My guys seeking my decisions and advice: 1.5 hours*
6. *Reading and replying to emails: 1.5 hours*
7. *Working on projects assigned by bosses: 2 hours*
8. *Attending discussions that my guys can handle: 1 hour.*
9. *Thinking about next steps: 0 ?????*

He quickly sums the hours up. Mama Mia! It's 13.5 hours. Amazingly, lunch time has not even been factored in. What's worse, he hasn't even spent a single minute planning ahead as a manager. Typically, he leaves for home at 10 p.m. It is a long journey back, and he always gets home very hungry and tired. The cycle repeats itself day after day.

It's increasingly clear to him that he is not in control of his work. On the contrary, his work is controlling him! What must he do differently? He looks up from the screen and gazes at other patrons streaming in for their morning cuppa.

Time is a precious commodity. Don't fritter it away.

Winston Churchill once said, "Failure to plan is planning to fail." Ironically, though Raja does a great job in planning his company's production schedule, he doesn't apply the same treatment to his workday. What he is experiencing, though unpleasant, is not uncommon. It is also not a new manager's phenomenon, I assure you. Managers very high up the corporate ladder and who prowl the corridors of power are similarly afflicted. The scene reminds us of hamsters running on wheels.

At this point, I would like to share with you a few useful tools and concepts that will help the likes of Raja get back on an even keel. As you apply these tools, you will no doubt devise others as well. Experiment with them and start to reap the benefits.

The importance of time management cannot be overestimated. If you do it right, it will serve you well for the rest of your career. You will accomplish much more in a shorter time and still have some bandwidth in reserve to take on things that are more far-reaching and strategic. This becomes of pivotal importance as you move up the corporate ladder. You will then be literally juggling ten balls of different sizes and shapes in the air simultaneously. Therefore, it's best for you to learn and master the basics now when all you have to do is juggle three balls, so to speak.

PLAN YOUR WORK AND WORK YOUR PLAN

There are three basic steps here:

1. Set up a To Do list
2. Assign priorities
3. Act on what your list says

The To Do list is simply a list of items that you have identified as needing your attention. At the end of each day, spend a few minutes to plan what you wish to do the following day. Prioritize the items and then make sure that you carry out your plan the next day. Review what you have accomplished at the end of the day, crossing out the completed items and adding new ones. The key is this: Plan your work and work your plan.

HOW TO PRIORITIZE

Not everything that comes to your mind is worth your time doing. Time is a precious commodity. To make the best use of it, we will need to know our priorities.

> *"Things that matter most must never be at the mercy*
> *of things that matter least."*
> — Goethe

A useful time management model is the Importance vs Urgency Matrix illustrated by Diagram 7.1. I first came across this in the *The Seven Habits of Highly Effective People* written by Stephen Covey.

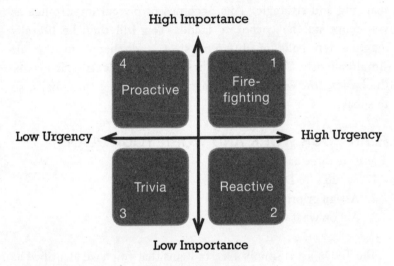

Diagram 7.1: The Importance vs Urgency Matrix

There are two dimensions to consider: urgency vs importance. When something is urgent, it presses on us and says "Do it now." It may not be important but it gives us a sense of accomplishment when we do it. Remember the time when your printer misbehaved while you were trying to print a report? Instead of calling for help from the company's IT department, you stopped everything and spent the next 30 minutes fixing it yourself. It felt good, didn't it when you finally got that darned thing to work?

When something is important, it has great impact on your results as a manager. It is usually also quite difficult to complete. Thus we tend to put important matters off because we tell ourselves that we need more time to do them properly.

In the matrix are four quadrants, namely: (1) Fire-fighting, (2) Reactive, (3) Trivia and (4) Proactive. Using this matrix, let's diagnose how Raja has been using or misusing his time. Chances are, Raja has been devoting nearly all his time in Quadrants 1, 2 and 3. As he has been so overwhelmed by these daily demands, he hardly has any time left for Quadrant 4.

Effective managers should consciously place as top priority the activities in Quadrant 4—the things that matter most. This is being forward-looking and proactive and ought to be the largest chunk of their workday. They do this by understanding the rhythm of their business. By knowing the peaks and troughs in the work year, they will observe how certain months are very action-packed and some weeks less so. They then orchestrate activities so that they and their team are doing what are important before they become urgent. By taking this approach, they will need to work less on tasks in Quadrants 1 and 2, and they will consciously waste no time in Quadrant 3—the things that matter least.

THE 80/20 PRINCIPLE

When we decide to work on a number of activities, it will pay off handsomely in terms of higher effectiveness if we take into account the 80/20 principle. This is also known as the Pareto's Law, named after Italian economist Vilfredo Pareto. Simply stated, it means that if we do 100 things, 80 percent of the desired results will come from only 20 percent of the things we do.

These are some examples that may resonate with you:
- 20 percent of your customer base may likely be responsible for 80 percent of your revenue;
- 20 percent of the actions you take may produce 80 percent of your results; or
- 20 percent of the emails you read may contribute to 80 percent of the information that you need.

Therefore, pause and think before acting. Not all activities are equally productive to engage in. Some are just more beneficial than others!

FINDING WHAT WORKS FOR YOU

In the previous sections, we discussed how to prioritize using the Importance vs Urgency matrix and the 80/20 principle. Although most people are familiar with them, finding a workable way to productively manage their time remains elusive.

The biggest rock that stands in their way is that the items in quadrant 1 are too numerous and daunting. Unless these are cut down to manageable proportions, they become overwhelmed by a sense of deja vu and helplessness. Why? Because it has been like this for a long time. And heaven knows they have tried to apply time management tools for the longest time. Yet, they can hardly keep their head above the water.

What are underlying causes? There are four keys ones that I'd like discuss here.

1.Lack of scrutiny of the items in Quadrant 1

When items are lumped into Quadrant 1, do we ask whether they really belong there in the first place? Probably not. We just assume that they should be there. This is the start of the downward spiral.

The emergency rooms of hospitals have to deal with patients who all seem to need immediate medical attention. Due to limited medical resources it's simply not possible to accord top priority to everybody. Through a system called triage, patients are quickly assessed and then sorted into different categories so that those with the most dire needs are treated ahead of those whose treatment can be delayed till later. .

The triage process can be applied to time management. All you need is to pause a little and ask yourselves some probing questions. This will enable you to move some items out. Your head starts to clear a little, and you can breathe easier.

2. Allowing others to dump their work into your Quadrant 1

In today's matrix organisation, it is quite common to have to respond to urgent calls for help from peers, stakeholders and bosses. Such exigencies are sometime unavoidable. But there are times when you know that with a little forward thinking of the part of your colleagues, these last minute surges could have been reduced. If you notice a pattern to such requests, it is incumbent upon you to bring this up and agree on a mutually acceptable way forward. There is an adage that speaks to this: You get what you tolerate.

3. Procrastination in addressing items in Quadrant 4

Items which are important but not urgent are usually ignored until they become urgent. If we envision a conveyor belt flowing from Quadrants 4 to 1, we realise immediately that it's inevitable that with the passage of time Quadrant 4 items will morph into Quadrant 1's.

When items are in Quadrant 4, we have time on our side. We can plan better and do a better job. This is right the place and time for managers and their teams to focus and do their best job. Their aim should be to stop the moving conveyor belt and not allow anything within their control to spill over to Quadrant 1.

Yet, many managers will procrastinate. Some have said, albeit tongue-in-cheek, that when there is time on their side, somehow the thrill is missing. You don't get that adrenaline rush that kicks in when you are dealing with a crisis. On a more sober note, they do concede that this is irresponsible leadership and is the quickest route to burnout and a demotivation.

The choice is yours.

4. Poor deployment of your resources

Managers who are constantly fire-fighting may be not be leveraging resources that are already available. A good manager multiplies his effectiveness through working with others. There are two ways he can do this. Firstly by developing his team members and raising their capabilities so that they can take on more. Secondly, it is through collaboration with others. In the rest of this book, we'll discuss these two topics.

IS MULTI-TASKING COOL?

These days, it is not uncommon for a manager to perform multiple tasks simultaneously: read emails, talk on the phone and gather her documents for a meeting that is about to take place. If you are one of these people, you will inevitably become highly stressed, frenzied, distracted and irritable.

By multi-tasking on a 24/7 basis, you risk overloading your brain. Instead of helping you become more productive, it will do the reverse. Gradually, the brain loses its capacity to focus fully and thoroughly on anything at one time. There is even a name for this real but unrecognized neurological phenomenon—attention deficit trait (ADT)[1], according to Dr. Edward Hallowell, a psychiatrist who specializes in cognitive and emotional health. The core symptoms are inner frenzy and difficulties in staying organized, setting priorities and managing time.

ADT is turning many otherwise gifted people into underperformers. Your brain will work better if you slow down a little and take one step at a time. Perhaps the idiom "More haste, less speed" bears more wisdom than we think.

WHAT DOES YOUR DIARY TELL YOU?

As a sanity check, look at your diary once in a while. For those on Microsoft Outlook, scan your calendar. A clear sign of trouble will be back-to-back meetings day after day. In other words, you have a chock-a-block schedule. Some may derive a perverse, almost masochistic, pleasure out of this as it shows and makes them feel that they are working very hard. In effect though, it is a plight not much different from that of a hamster on its wheel. Who's running the show? The hamster or the wheel?

I recommend that you think long and hard about this. Start to clear the deck, so to speak. It is good practice to have some white space in your diary. It may be just a 30-minute slot.

Use it to catch a breather and get some perspective. Also, it acts as a buffer in case someone wants to meet you to discuss something important. This could be a subordinate who needs help urgently. Nothing turns your people off more than to know that you are fully booked and they will have to wait till the next month to see you.

END-OF-DAY REFLECTION

Set aside a few minutes to reflect at the end of the day. What have you done today? Are there things that you did which perhaps should not have been done? Managers who are always on the go and have endless items on their To Do list are doing themselves and their people no favour, to put it mildly. Less is sometimes more. The Chinese have a phrase for this—*wei wu wei*—which literally reads "doing not doing". Let's remember to slow down in order to speed up.

Very importantly, connect with your family. Allocate some time for yourself to do what will nourish your soul. Do some exercise, relax and get adequate sleep. Soon, you will begin each day with a spring in your step and a fresh perspective that comes only when the body and mind have been recharged. We'll discuss more about this in Chapter 25.

- Failure to plan is planning to fail.
- Before rushing to act, think about the 80/20 principle.

Q1: Refer to the Importance vs Urgency matrix. Why will working on tasks or issues in Quadrant 4 reduce the need to work on Quadrants 1 and 2? Is there any harm in ignoring matters in Quadrant 3?

Q2: If you were Raja in the anecdote, how will you prioritize your workday now so that you can enhance your productivity significantly?

Q3: When you faced with too many items in Quadrant 4, how can you make them more manageable?

PART THREE
Managing Team Members

2. Managing Team Members	3. Managing Teams
1. Managing Yourself	
4. Managing Key Relationships	5. Becoming A More Complete Leader

"If you want one year of prosperity, cultivate grains.
If you want ten years of prosperity, cultivate trees.
If you want one hundred years of prosperity, cultivate people."
—Chinese proverb

✳8 LEADERSHIP IS A RELATIONSHIP

STARTING OFF ON THE RIGHT FOOTING

What are some things that you should do on your first few days as the manager? If you have been promoted from within the organization, you have an edge compared to the person who has been recruited from outside. To start with, you will be more familiar with the corporate culture. And, before you assume your new role you will likely have had a few dialogues with your would-be boss.

In any case, having a meaningful conversation with your new boss will be the first order of business. These are some of the areas that you may wish to bring up:

- What is her vision for the organization that she is heading up? What are her key objectives, priorities and Key Performance Indicators or KPIs?
- What does she expect of the managers reporting to her?
- What does she expect of you?
- How does she view the dynamics of her management team—you and your peers? (e.g. Collaboration? Openness? Trust?)
- What are her views of the department that you are now leading? Are there areas that are of concern to her?
- What is her preferred way for you to work with her?

Once you have had this conversation, the next set of stakeholders you will need to speak with will be your subordinates and peers. It is difficult to overestimate the importance of building a healthy relationship with them.

As a manager, your subordinates are crucial to your success. Without them, you are reduced to a team of one person. It is impossible for one person to accomplish what a team can do.

When you're able to win the hearts and minds of your team members, you are able to multiply the fruits of your labour.

Peers are just as important for you. In this age where matrix reporting is becoming the norm, we need the support of our peers as much as they need ours. There will be many occasions when having the backing of your peers will make a difference between success and failure.

I will have more to say about managing your relationship with your bosses and peers in Part Five. Throughout the rest of this chapter, we shall focus on building that all-important relationship with your subordinates.

We start by listening in on the conversation between Kim, a newly appointed department head, and Joon, his subordinate.

Managerial Anecdote

Kim used to be part of a four-member team in a department. Recently, the department head was assigned to the New York office as part of the company's leadership development programme. Before that announcement was made, the GM of the division invited Kim for a chat and informed him that he would be promoted to department manager.

On Kim's first day as the new manager, he met with his team members—three former peers and one new person transferred from another department. It had gone well and all the people present were attentive and quite relaxed about the change of leadership. They all congratulated him on his promotion.

Kim, however, sensed that one team member was very quiet. He seemed to be lost in his own thoughts. This person was Joon. In the last three years, there had been a few bouts of friction between both Kim and Joon. Both were standouts in the department and were considered the most creative and productive in the company. While Kim was usually composed and empathetic, Joon was intense and impatient.

Now that the company had promoted Kim, it was likely that Joon was concerned about his own future. Putting himself in Joon's shoes, Kim realized that it was necessary to meet and clear up any misunderstanding that might have existed between them.

Kim walked over to Joon's workspace and asked him whether he would be available to join him for lunch. Although a little surprised by the gesture, Joon accepted quite readily.

The lunch meeting turned out very well. Both men were very open and shared their thoughts about what had happened in the past. They even had a few laughs when they both admitted that they had harboured no ill-feelings towards each other. It was all in the spirit of constructive conflict, a practice that their company valued highly.

That lunch meeting was the start of a strong partnership between them. By discussing differences that had once divided them, they had now begun to appreciate each other more. The leadership that both exhibited set the tone for the rest of the department. A year later, Joon was promoted to head up another department in the company.

A key success factor:
your relationship with your subordinates

Working with countless managers in various parts of the world, I do notice that those who are outstanding all have excellent relationships with their subordinates. This shouldn't come as a surprise. Although hardly a day passes without news of how the world has become surrounded by a web of networking technologies such as Twitter and Facebook, when it comes to people working with one another, nothing can supplant the old-fashioned relationship.

> *"Leadership is a relationship between those who aspire*
> *to lead and those who choose to follow."*
> — Kouzes and Posner
> Authors of *The Leadership Challenge*

In the managerial anecdote that you have just read, Kim knew how important it was to connect with his team members on his first day as their manager. And this was exactly what he did. You might even call it a kind of ritual for new managers

First, he met them all as a team, and talked about how pleased and honoured he was to be working with them. If team members didn't know him, he would introduce himself and share a little about himself as a person and his background. Then he might have invited each person to say something about herself and anything on her mind. After that, Kim would likely have shared the key points of his conversation with his boss, including what her expectations were.

As these were his first days as the manager, Kim might only be able to touch lightly on objectives and priorities. He should probably mention that he intended to organize regular team meetings to get aligned and coordinated. Also, he would really like to spend time with each member of the team one-on-one to establish a greater understanding and to discuss how to best work with each other.

And in the days ahead, he would be meeting each team member in an informal fashion. It could even be over a cup of tea or over lunch. Starting off a working relationship on a more casual footing puts people at ease and is highly recommended.

Keep the initial conversation relatively short, say, no more than 45 minutes. You may consider:

- Saying something about yourself. You may expand on what you had already shared at the team meeting. This is a good way to get connected. You don't have to tell your life history. But do reveal something personal, such as funny stories about your family and hobbies.
- Inviting the other party to do the same.
- Saying something about your personal values and about work.
- Then asking them to share about what is important to them.
- Discussing generally your objectives and priorities for the department.

This is only the start of many one-on-one conversations between you and the people who work with you. As you get to know one another, a sense of mutual trust will gradually be apparent.

CREATE A SAFE ENVIRONMENT
FOR EXCHANGE OF IDEAS

Listening is a powerful leadership competency. When you listen to others patiently, you are saying to them that you respect them and are interested in what they have to say. This is an invitation to them to come forward and say whatever is on their mind. Make it safe for them to do so.

In time, you will discover more and more about your people—their world views, values, what motivates them, their strengths and blind spots. And this will provide leads on how you may help them become even more effective.

After each conversation, write down some brief notes that you may refer to later. This will come in handy as you prepare for the next conversation some weeks from now. Also, it acts as a reminder of actions that you have committed to do, and what the other person has agreed to do.

I have come across managers who gradually turn the regular one-on-one sessions into a work review meeting. If this happens, your people will soon dread it. As mentioned, be generous. Devote ample time to work, but consciously set aside some time for the person in front of you to share his or her thoughts with you.

Asian subordinates in general need time to warm up to their bosses. In turn, Asian bosses are themselves rather reticent and unwilling to spend time one-on-one with their people. However, I have witnessed situations where bosses reach out to their subordinates and succeed in breaking the ice with them. That's when the real dialogue and exchange of ideas begin.

In many parts of Asia, such as China, Taiwan, Hong Kong, Japan, Korea, Singapore, Malaysia, Thailand, Vietnam etc, people tend to be modest and reserved. At company conferences, while their American and European dominate these conversations, these Asians tend to stay in the background and patiently wait to be invited to share their opinions. There is also a Chinese saying, *"tao guang yang hui"*, which means "to hide one's capabilities and not let others know what one knows".

There are two key takeaways here for bosses and subordinates respectively. Bosses need to take the first step in creating a safe environment for their people to speak up. For subordinates, they need to realize that ideas are the new currency of the 21st century. They will do themselves a great disservice if they insist on hiding their capabilities and not articulating their points of view. We'll have more on this in Chapter 24. Perhaps it's time to realize that the spirit of *"tao guang yang hui"* has become irrelevant and passé.

HOW TO BUILD TRUST

How the relationship between you and each of your subordinates evolves will very much depend on the trust that is gradually developing. Just as you wish to win the other person's trust, he or she will need to earn yours as well.

People will start to develop trust in one another only if, in the course of their relationship, they are convinced that the following characteristics are present in the other party:

- **Competence:** Knowledge, skills and judgment to perform the work.
- **Character:** This is synonymous with integrity and honesty.
- **Authenticity:** How genuine each person is.
- **Consistency:** Walking the talk by doing what has been committed.

Trust is essential to effective leadership communication and teamwork. When it exists, decisions are made at a faster pace because people have the confidence that everyone is working in the team's best interest. Productivity improves and the relationship is inspiring and serves as a source of competitive advantage. The climate is more open and vibrant, with a free flow of ideas. Greater risk-taking and innovation will result.

In contrast, when trust is lacking, work slows down. People are plagued with doubts. They are fearful of hidden agendas and will be concerned about protecting their flanks. Personal and team productivity will suffer.

BALANCING SOFT AND HARD POWER[1]

When you earn the trust of your people as a leader, you have acquired soft power. People are drawn towards you because in you they see someone who possesses competence, character, authenticity and consistency.

Leaders will of course need hard power as well. Essentially, this comes from your position as a manager. For instance, each time you decide which assignments to delegate to your people, it is an exercise of your hard power as their boss. Another example will be the painful but sometimes necessary task of reprimanding an employee who has acted in an irresponsible manner.

Effective managers are able to combine both hard and soft power. This results in smart power. They are aware that purely exercising one to the exclusion of the other will create problems for themselves at the workplace.

- Trust is the foundation of leadership. Trust is earned only when people demonstrate the following characteristics: competence, character, authenticity and consistency.

- Effective managers exercise smart power by combining both soft and hard power.

Q1: Look at leaders who you know. How much do you trust them? How does that influence your relationship with them at work?

Q2: What are some situations that you have come across where hard power needs to be exercised? How have you handled such situations yourself?

9 HOW TO DELEGATE

WHY DELEGATE?
As managers we can't do everything ourselves. That's not what we are hired to do. Our job is to leverage resources at our disposal and orchestrate the successful accomplishment of a variety of activities. Hence, we need to know how to delegate effectively. If it is done well, the benefits are many:

- Important tasks are completed efficiently and in a coordinated fashion by various team members;
- Valuable time is freed up for higher value-added activities that managers are expected by their bosses to handle; and
- It is a great way to develop team members for greater responsibilities.

COMMON PROBLEMS IN DELEGATION
Unfortunately, for all its merits, delegation is frequently not done well. These are some common difficulties faced:

- Assignments delegated are either unfulfilled or executed unsatisfactorily;
- Managers are unwilling to delegate because they think their people aren't capable;
- Some managers delegate the tasks, and then interfere and micromanage;
- Managers fear that they will lose control and power through delegation;
- Subordinates are unwilling to accept the responsibilities because they lack confidence and capability;
- Some managers view delegation as a legitimate way of getting rid of what they perceive to be low-level and menial tasks that they dump onto subordinates;

- When assignments are delegated, managers do not follow up and provide support. Essentially, they abdicate through delegation;
- Subordinates lack trust in their managers and are sceptical of their superiors' ways and intentions (e.g. managers who abandon their team members after delegating and return only to claim credit for themselves when the work's done);
- Subordinates are bitter and unhappy with being part of, or contributing to, the success of the team whose manager was a peer previously.

TWO KEY PRINCIPLES TO BEAR IN MIND

1. Managers may delegate but they are still responsible for the overall outcome. Hence, they can't abdicate.
2. To delegate effectively and responsibly, guidance is required from the managers. The nature of the guidance provided will depend on the tasks and the subordinate's developmental stage.

HOW TO GUIDE WHEN YOU DELEGATE

When managers delegate, they frequently wonder to what extent they need to stay involved with their subordinates. Should they follow through very closely or should they take a hands-off approach after delegation?

Yet another concern is about being consistent in the way they relate to each subordinate. For instance, if they have decided to do a close follow-up with one subordinate, in the interest of consistency, shouldn't they apply the same treatment to all the others in the team? This speaks to the time-honoured notion of fairness, i.e. treat everybody the same.

You will have the answers to both questions if you do a diagnosis of the subordinate's developmental stage before you delegate. A person's developmental stage depends on the interplay of two factors: skill and will. Let's now review the following diagram.

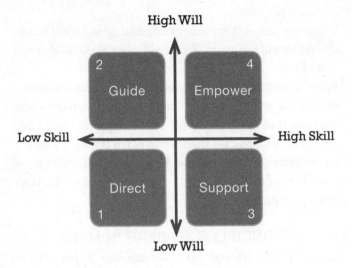

High Will

| 2 | | 4 |
| Guide | | Empower |

Low Skill ← → High Skill

| | Direct | | Support | |
| 1 | | | 3 |

Low Will

Diagram 9.1: The Skill/Will Matrix[1]

In this matrix, "skill" will be a composite of a person's knowledge, training and experience. "Will" depends on the person's motivation, drive, attitude and ambition.

There are four developmental stages[2] as depicted in the diagram. They are as follows:

Developmental Stage One: Low Skill/Low Will

A person at this stage is likely to be someone who does not have the necessary skills and knowledge for the job and hence lacks confidence. She is understandably reluctant as she does not want to come up short of your expectations.

Her needs are two-fold: Firstly the know-how to get things done, and secondly as she starts to make progress, she needs you to let her know that she is meeting your expectations.

The style to adopt towards her is to **Direct**. Spend time with her and establish a mutual understanding on what the assignment entails. Invite her to share her concerns and assure her that you will provide her the support to get the job accomplished.

Identify an assignment that is relatively straightforward for a start. Brief her thoroughly and give detailed instructions. Follow through closely and provide feedback on how she is doing. You will find that as she progresses, she will lighten up somewhat and become more self-confident. In the next assignment, pick something similar and loosen up a little in terms of supervision. Hopefully, she may move to Stage Two soon.

Someone who is at this stage may possibly be a misfit for the role. If you are convinced that this is the case, it is best to speak to her openly and do what is best for the individual and the company. In some cases, it may be an exit strategy.

Developmental Stage Two: Low Skill/High Will

This person is likely to be a newcomer to the company. Though lacking in knowledge and expertise, she is enthusiastic and is willing to learn. Do note that when a person is overly enthusiastic, she may bite off more than she can chew. She doesn't know what she doesn't know.

Her need is to acquire more experience and insights. When you delegate an assignment to such a person, the aim is to provide her more exposure and challenges so that she will acquire greater maturity in judgment.

The approach to take towards her is to **Guide**. This is a blend of providing the know-how while broadening her awareness of important factors to consider. Encourage her to ask questions. Invite suggestions from her, and provide her some room to make mistakes in a safe way. In other words, create conditions for her to learn from the school of hard knocks, so to speak.

Developmental Stage Three: High Skill/Low Will

At this developmental stage, the subordinate has acquired considerable knowledge and competence. While you are convinced that she is ready for bigger things, she may not think so. There may be a variety of reasons for this. One possibility is that the subordinate now realizes that with the experience acquired, her boss has higher expectations and will expect more. Another possibility may be that the subordinate may have recently suffered a set-back in her work and is still smarting from it. In both instances, she is starting to have self-doubts.

Her need is to acquire or regain self-confidence. The style to adopt towards her is to **Support**. This means encouraging her and giving her the boost that she will need. There is really no need to provide more know-how. She's got this already.

Developmental Stage Four: High Skill/High Will
With the passage of time, the subordinate has achieved considerable success and self-confidence. Not only is she capable, she is also someone whom others look up to. You have a lot of respect for her judgment and are convinced that she can operate independently. In fact, you would like her to take on even larger responsibilities. Possibly, she may be ready to be promoted.

At this stage, such a person needs more challenging projects. She is keen to prove that she is ready for a bigger role. To spur her further, identify stretch assignments for her. Allow her room to operate autonomously and have full accountability. The style to adopt is to **Empower**.

HOW TO DELEGATE EFFECTIVELY
You will find yourself delegating more effectively when you:
- Know each of your subordinates. What are their experiences and expertise? Identify their individual developmental stages.
- Identify an assignment that will match your subordinate's developmental stage. The assignment should facilitate her growth in terms of equipping her with more skills and/ or will.
- Have a conversation with the subordinate. Discuss the requirements and ensure an alignment in expectations is achieved.

- Highlight the developmental nature of the assignment. For instance, this may require her to work with co-workers in other functions. By taking this on, it will sharpen her ability to influence without formal authority. Gauge her willingness and appetite for this assignment. Secure her buy-in and commitment.
- Discuss how you will support her. Agree on the frequency of progress reviews.
- Debrief at the end of the assignment. Extract the lessons learnt. Celebrate your subordinate's success.

See Appendix One for an example of how one manager first diagnoses his subordinate's developmental stage and then identifies an assignment that will accelerate her growth. Now, back to the point about treating everybody the same. Should you interact with all your subordinates the same way then?

The answer is clearly a "No". When it comes to delegation and development, treat your people as individuals. Remember the maxim: "Different strokes for different folks."

LET GO AND LET GROW

When your people are running into some difficulties, as a good boss, you may be tempted to jump in and provide relief. But pause and think before reacting. Remind yourself that by intervening too quickly to save your people, you may be stunting their growth.

Picture yourself teaching a three-year-old child to ride a bike. Will he ever learn to ride confidently on his own if you are always there holding on? Learning comes only after some falls and bruises are sustained.

> *"A gem cannot be polished without friction;*
> *nor a man perfected without trials."*
> —Old Chinese saying

Do expect that there will be delays and productivity losses at the beginning when your subordinates are doing something new. Have faith and exercise patience. Do you believe in them? Make no mistake about it. This is as much a test for you as it is for them.

DON'T CARRY YOUR SUBORDINATES' MONKEYS[3]

There will be subordinates who have a habit of attempting upward delegation. For instance, the moment they run into some difficulty, they will come running to you for help.

Be wary of this. Some managers do not handle this well. Flattered by the pleas for help, they willingly take on what is rightfully the subordinates' responsibility. Suddenly, like a monkey, the assignment leaps from the subordinate's shoulder to the boss's. Before long, other subordinates will get wind of how kind and helpful the boss. That's when the boss will have a whole zoo of wild animals leaping on his or her back.

Learn to recognize when someone is about to pass his monkey to you. Do not instinctively say, "Okay, let me look into this and I'll get back to you." Instead, say this, "Let's figure out what you can do on your own to tackle this challenge."

There are of course times when your people really need your help because a particular issue is just too tough for them to handle on their own. Once you are convinced about this, help them by all means. But do get them involved so that they can learn how to tackle this the next time. This is another opportunity to develop your people.

- Managers need to delegate so that they can be more effective in discharging their responsibilities. It is also a good way of developing their people.

- To delegate effectively and responsibly, guidance is required from the managers. The nature of the guidance depends on the tasks and the subordinate's development stage. Apply different strokes for different folks.

Q1: Assess the developmental stages of your subordinates.

Q2: What is your delegation strategy to help them develop further?

10   THE MANAGER AS COACH

THE ARGUMENTS AGAINST COACHING
Many managers struggle with the notion that they need to coach their people. There are two arguments they have against this:

1. They were never coached by their bosses. Yet they have been able to learn things on their own and are obviously pretty successful. So why should they coach their people?

2. It is so time-consuming. Sitting down to coach someone requires a lot of patience and takes up precious time. And what irks them further is that despite this effort, the subordinate may still be unable to accomplish the work to the quality that is expected. And so they conclude, "Why waste time? If I do the work on my own, it is not only much faster but also better."

WHY MANAGERS SHOULD COACH
When I discuss coaching, I usually say upfront that coaching is not entirely an act of altruism. It is also because of enlightened self-interest. Why so? Because as managers we need to work through our people. If we have capable and motivated people on our teams, our work gets done more efficiently and we achieve the success that we desire. Otherwise, we'll struggle and work very long hours doing what our people should be doing. And because of that, we won't have time for more strategic matters that we may need to focus on. This will ultimately mean that we won't be giving to our organization the values that they expect of us.

In a nutshell, there are four compelling reasons for coaching your people:
   • It is a social responsibility of all managers to invest in developing their people. If our bosses did little to develop

us in the past, it does not mean we should perpetuate their act of omission. Managers are part of a privileged group. By passing on our learning, we contribute to a better workplace and society.

- It raises the capabilities of your people. When they become successful, you become successful.
- You will develop a reputation as a developer of people and become a magnet for talent. And if you look around, you will notice that highly successful leaders attract great people to their teams.
- You will free up time to focus on the higher value-added activities that a manager needs to deliver. This is how you can make a more impactful contribution towards the overall objectives of your organization.

All these benefits will accrue only if you make the investment in time and effort upfront. Let's now address the second argument against coaching. This is best done by studying the methods adopted by two managers, Michael and Julian.

Managerial Anecdotes

Michael is a long-serving manager who has risen from the ranks. He has never been coached in all his career. Two years ago, he became the manager of a team of service engineers. To him, the best way of getting things done is to issue clear directions to his people and have them come back to him regularly for more clarification if they are unclear. He applies this same approach to all five engineers.

It seems to work well. Things get done and he is always on top of the situation. Though he is involved knee-deep in all the nitty-gritty, he doesn't mind. Most days he comes to work very early in the morning and is never home until very late at night when all his children are already in bed.

If you talk to him, he frequently laments his engineers' lack of ability to think and act independently. Though they are relatively experienced, they seem constantly in need of guidance and assurance. In truth, he is rather disappointed that after two years of hand-holding from him, he is still as busy as when he first became a manager. His boss has been asking him to delegate and let go so that he can take on other responsibilities. But alas, how can he do that? It seems to him things will surely fall apart because his engineers just aren't ready. Letting go seems too risky a venture for him.

Julian has recently been promoted to manage a team of three accountants. Before his promotion, he attended a programme to equip managers with coaching skills. He is therefore keen to put these skills to work.

He has spent quite a lot of time establishing a trusting relationship with each of his subordinates. They are all relatively inexperienced, none having had more than a year on the job. Whenever he assigns them a piece of work, he will spend time providing the necessary background information, and define what the expectations are. He also makes time for his people to ask questions. They then agree on how frequently there will be follow-up sessions to check on the work progress.

When his people come back to him for clarification, he has sometimes been tempted to just tell them what to do and get on with it. Perhaps, that may hasten the pace of work. Fortunately, he has been able to restrain himself. Instead, he asks them questions and encourages them to think of their own solutions. If they are really stuck, he will offer suggestions though. "Oooh...," he groans, "it's so time-consuming." But he persists.

This process has been continuing for more than six months. And slowly but surely, he notices a change in his people. They are more self-assured now. When he delegates a piece of work now, they react quite confidently and will ask some pointed questions to ensure alignment in terms of expectations and outcomes. Then they are off on their own. During their periodic progress reviews, the work will have advanced considerably in the right direction.

Julian is a happy camper these days. He continues to coach his people but they seem to need much less attention from him. With the spare time freed up, he plans ahead. His boss has complimented him for being proactive. His team is performing very well and their morale is the highest in the company.

Let's first do a quick diagnosis of these two different styles of management.

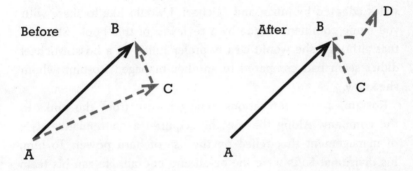

Before — B — After — B — D

Michael's style: AB
Julian's style: ACB

Michael's style: AB
Julian's style: CBD

Diagram 10.1: Two styles of management

In the beginning, Michael's directive style (AB) is more efficient, while Julian's coaching approach (ACB) is very time-consuming. As you can see, ACB is a crooked line and is longer than AB which is the straight line between A and B.

Sometime later, the situation has flipped around. While Michael continues with his directive style, his people have gone no further. They are still stuck at A. In contrast, Julian's people have gained in competence and experience. They are now at C. Getting from C to B is a shorter and faster route than from A to B. And Julian now has extra time to focus on more strategic activities from B to D.

Doesn't this remind you of the fable of the hare and the tortoise racing each other? Julian, the tortoise, has had a slow start but at mid-point he surpasses Michael, the hare, and leaves him in the dust.

"Give a man a fish, he eats for a day.
Teach him how to fish, he eats for a lifetime."
— Old Chinese saying

Before we conclude our discussions about the two different styles adopted by Julian and Michael, I would like to share with you some comments made by a reviewer of this book. She said that although she would clearly prefer Julian as a boss, Michael didn't seem bad compared to another manager, Rostam, whom she knew.

Rostam, a communications manager, rose from the ranks in the company. Along the way, he acquired a manipulative style of management that relied on the use of hard power. To him, his divisional KPIs were the be-all and end-all. He ran his team like a "pompous dictator", coercing them to produce results at all cost. Distant and dismissive, he soon lost touch with what was happening around him. Whenever his subordinates came to him with queries, he was frequently unable to provide any guidance. He would resort to an old trick: throw the question back to his people. Then he would declare, "A good coach never provides answers. My questions are to challenge you to think on your own!"

Left on their own, his people ploughed on. Although they did meet the targets set, they became increasingly disenchanted and resentful that their boss was reaping huge bonuses by cracking the whip from the comfort of his desk.

SO WHAT IS COACHING REALLY?
The purpose of coaching is to enable others to discover solutions for themselves. It is different from teaching or training. In training

or teaching, the spotlight is on the teacher or trainer. He is the person with knowledge and expertise to impart. He tells the learner what he needs to know and the learner takes it all in. Usually, the interaction is one way: from the teacher /trainer to the learner.

In contrast, a coaching relationship adopts a learner-centric approach. The spotlight is on the coachee. The coach does not play the role of an expert. He is a dialogue partner whose main purpose is to facilitate discovery of solutions through thought-provoking questions. By being an empathetic listener, the coach creates a safe place for the coachee to share what is on his mind. This is key to facilitating the coachee's learning as he will learn best when there is encouragement to raise questions and express his own opinions. In this way, the exchange becomes dynamic and two-way. Through this process, the coachee actively explores various options, and then comes to a conclusion about what works and what does not.

At the end of a good coaching conversation, both the coach and coachee should feel that something meaningful has taken place. The coachee has greater clarity of what he wishes to do and is committed to making it a reality.

HOW TO COACH: THE GROW MODEL[1]

How does one conduct a coaching conversation? I would like to introduce a simple and easy to use framework called The GROW Model. It consists of four steps. In the description below I will refer to the manager as the coach and the co-worker as the coachee.

Step 1: Goal

Discuss and agree with coachee on the topic and objectives of the discussion.

As a simple example, let's say that the coachee is habitually late in submitting a sales status report at the end of the week. The goal is to help him identify and take actions to submit his report on time.

Step 2: Reality
Ask the coachee what the current situation is.
He acknowledges that his report is usually late by an hour. He is aware that the deadline is 3 p.m. on Friday.

Step 3: Options
Between the Goal and the Reality, is the Gap. What are some possible options to bridge the gap?
The coachee is encouraged to come up with his own options. Some of his suggestions are: (a) Start working on the report the day before and not wait till Friday morning when he gets overwhelmed by other urgent work, (b) ... (c)...

Step 4: Way Forward
Among the options discussed, what appear most practical? Are there any obstacles that may prevent him from taking any of the options? If so, what does he need to do? When will he implement his plan?
At the end of Step 4 there needs to be a commitment on actions. A coaching session is meaningful only if an action plan is the result. In the days ahead, the coachee will turn his action plan into reality.

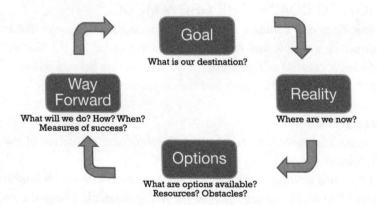

Diagram 10.2: The GROW Model

The four-step framework is easy to understand and apply. However, to be an effective coach, we need more than just a framework. Owning a sleek-looking set of golf clubs, for example, does not make one a good golfer. In both situations, we need certain proficiencies. We will talk more about these in the next chapter.

- Coaching is not an entirely altruistic act. Both the managers and their subordinates will derive immense mutual benefits.

- The GROW model is a simple and practical framework for a coaching conversation.

Q1: According to Rostam, "A good coach never provides answers!" Do you agree with him?

Q2: When you coach, what steps can you take to help the coachee learn how to fish and feed himself?

11   COACHING PROFICIENCIES

BEFORE STARTING TO COACH...

In order to be able to coach effectively, you not only need a framework for coaching, but also a set of proficiencies. They are as follows:

• Trust- and Rapport-Building
• Listening
• Questioning
• Giving feedback
• Use of silence
• Acknowledgement/Celebration

Trust- and Rapport-Building

Before even attempting to coach a co-worker, there needs to be a certain level of trust and comfort between you and the other party. Otherwise, the conversation will be contrived and superficial.

You will also have another hurdle to overcome—subordinates are generally not enthused with the idea of sitting down and having conversations with their bosses. It reminds them of performance appraisal sessions, which are always stressful.

So how do you reach the point when your people are ready to be coached? It's a gradual process.

First of all, trust and rapport need to be built. A mutually trusting relationship is the precursor for a fruitful coaching relationship. That's the subject of our discussion in Chapter 8: "Leadership is a Relationship".

Listening

Listening is a lost art.[1] Somehow, in the course of acquiring a formal education and growing up, we have seemingly forgotten how to listen. It is a global phenomenon. Very commonly, when we are "listening" to another person, countless thoughts are racing through our minds.

We are fidgeting and our lips are ready to part. And the moment the other party finishes saying his piece, out comes our rejoinder at the speed of light.

This is not listening. Neither is this a conversation. It is more like a tennis match between two arch-rivals, lobbing volleys at each other.

Thousands of years ago, people in China discovered the secrets of real listening. Let's look at the character for the word "Listening" in the traditional Chinese script.

Ears   Eyes

King   Heart

Diagram 11.1: Listening

To be a good listener, we must first recognize that the most important moment is now. The most important person is the person in our presence. He is the king, so to speak. We will devote full attention to him by silencing all inner chatter. By engaging our ears, eyes and heart, the true meaning of what is being said will become very clear to us.

Questioning

Do recall that when you are coaching, you aren't playing the role of an expert. As an expert, you tell. When you tell, what is the impact on the person you are coaching? Telling implies that you hold the key, and that you know more than the coachee. You have suddenly thrown a wrench into the mutually respectful and open relationship that you have tried to cultivate. The free exchange of ideas now grounds to a halt. Is that what you want as a coach?

"The manager of the past knew how to tell.
The manager of the future knows how to ask."
— Peter Drucker

By asking questions, you are inviting the other person to explore options for tackling the challenges that he is grappling with. Through showing empathy and patience, the environment is transformed into a safe haven for ideas to flow freely in. It is in this state that the coachee starts to contemplate solutions that previously he would have dismissed outright. Haven't we had moments when we were relaxed or unguarded, and suddenly an improbable idea sprang to our minds? Such ideas may be the solutions that we are looking for.

Ask open-ended questions as opposed to closed-ended questions. Open-ended questions are expansive and lead to infinite possibilities. They start with: what, why, when, how, where and who. Examples are: **What** would you like to achieve? **Why** is this of interest to you? **When** can we expect it to arrive? **How** can we overcome this? **Where** is the bottleneck? **Who** can we work with?

Closed-ended questions impose limitations on the range of responses. They reduce answers into "either-or" options: yes or no, right or wrong, 1 or 2. When you ask such questions, you are leading the discussions into the narrow end of the funnel. Examples of closed-ended questions are: Do you prefer option 1 or option 2? Is this right or wrong? Do you agree with my suggestion or not?

Giving feedback

In the course of a coaching conversation you may need to give feedback occasionally. It can't be just an endless series of questions. Otherwise, it becomes very much like an interrogation session.

Feedback may be required for another reason: your coachee is stuck. He can't see what is holding him back. You can. And you will need to jolt him out of this by saying something direct and forceful to him while still respecting him as a person.

For instance, you may say, "I notice that you are still very hesitant to take actions. What are you concerned about?"

I will have more to say about giving feedback in Chapter 12.

Use of silence

When two old friends come together to drink tea and chat, their conversation is frequently punctuated by bouts of silence. When there is silence, both people remain relaxed and comfortable. When the conversation resumes, new ideas and perspectives emerge, taking their conversation to greater heights.

In coaching or any other conversation, we need to be mindful that occasional pauses are useful. People in our modern age dread these and become nervous. They quickly say something to break the silence. In Eastern societies such as Japan, Korea and China, there is a high comfort level with silence.

In Japanese, the word *ma* means an interval or pause. In the art of effective listening, we, too, can use *ma*. This is when we can attend to the non-verbal cues that the other person is sending. Is he relaxed or tense? What does his tone tell us? Words convey the informational content, but what's the emotional content, which is even more important?

You may also pause when you are conversing with the other party. Stay cool, lean back slightly and be relaxed. Provide the space for thoughts to materialize and opinions to be formed. Done with finesse, silence is indeed golden.

Acknowledgement/Celebration

People who work with us all need acknowledgement when they have done something well or to the best of their abilities. This uplifts their spirit and spurs them on to take the next step. At work when our colleagues reach certain milestones in the course of an important project, we should also break from our routine and have a small celebration. And so it is for a coaching engagement. Your coachee has just done something significant. When she tells you about it, congratulate her and let her know how pleased you are. Do it with sincerity. It will matter to her.

ATTRIBUTES/QUALITIES OF A GOOD COACH

A good coach has many qualities similar to those of a good manager. These are some key ones:

- Self-aware
- Confident
- Approachable
- Patient
- Generous; believes in others' potential
- Authentic
- Open and receptive
- Always learning and improving
- A good role model

BALANCING YOUR ROLES
AS MANAGER AND COACH

Do note that you need to differentiate between two roles that you are playing as a manager and as a coach. If you don't know where to draw the line, you will get conflicted. So will your people.

My suggestion is for you to visualize yourself wearing two hats. Most of the time, you should wearing the hat of a manager. When you are about to embark on a coaching conversation, you need to be clear that you are changing hats. It might even be useful to say this to the other party, "Shall we now work on this situation as a coaching conversation?"

At the beginning when you are beginning to coach, such a demarcation will prevent a confusion over what role you are playing. As a manager, there will be times when you are under pressure and need things done quickly. On such occasions, it is not the time to coach. You will have to do what managers need to do.

Overtime, as you become more and more proficient both as a manager and as a coach, you will develop a natural balance between managing and coaching. The line becomes blurred and you will be able to do both seamlessly.

LEARNING HOW TO COACH

Learning how to coach is a long process. It can't be done overnight. Be patient with yourself and take it one step at a time. It is useful to bear in mind the following points:

- When you start coaching, select someone who is keen to be coached. Perhaps, partner up with a fellow manager to do peer coaching. Or if you are starting with a subordinate, choose someone who is receptive and ready to be coached.
- Select a comfortable environment for coaching. Keep it informal. Do it over a cup of tea. If you need to do it in your office, do not do it with you sitting behind your desk. This is the traditional boss-subordinate interaction and can only cause discomfort. Sit facing each other with no barrier between you and the other party.
- Keep the sessions short. Perhaps no more than 20 minutes for a start.
- You don't have to complete the entire GROW process in one sitting. It's fine to do it in a few sessions.
- You may not even need to keep using GROW as the framework. Sometimes, by listening well and asking good questions in a meeting, you may help someone to move along. Good coaching occurs when people who are being coached do not even realize it.
- Not everybody can be coached. Some people think that it is a poor use of time and prefer to be told what to do. Recognize who these people are, and don't attempt to coach them. Your time can be more productively spent elsewhere.

- The following proficiencies are required for coaching: (a)Trust- and Rapport-Building, (b) Listening, (c) Questioning, (d) Giving feedback, (e) Use of silence and (f) Acknowledgement/Celebration. Practise each of them at work.

- It is necessary to strike a balance between being a manager and a coach.

Q1: You now know the GROW Model as well as the proficiencies required for coaching. And it's time for us to observe a coaching conversation. Please turn to Appendix One.

Q2: How ready are you now to begin coaching? What are the first steps you would take?

12   GIVING FEEDBACK *

WHY MANAGERS MUST GIVE FEEDBACK

It's no secret that giving feedback is a very difficult act. Most people associate it to the dreaded once-a-year performance appraisal with their bosses where the verdict will be delivered on how well or poorly they have fared.

Yet, feedback is fundamentally one of the most important tools for managers to raise performance levels and to foster learning in the team. A McKinsey & Company survey[1] of over 12,000 managers throughout the world revealed that managers consider "candid, insightful feedback" extremely important to their development, but most say that their bosses aren't doing a good job in providing such feedback.

This finding parallels my experience in coaching managers who frequently tell me that they wish bosses will provide them more genuine and objective feedback on how they can improve.

DIFFICULTIES OF GIVING FEEDBACK

We aren't talking about Asian managers in particular. It is a world-wide phenomenon. Their counterparts in the United States and Europe do not find it any easier to give feedback as well. These are some key roadblocks that stand in the way:

- Fear of causing a hostile reaction
- Unprepared to deal with emotional outburst
- Belief that it will sour relationship as "face" will be lost
- Just don't know how to give feedback
- Personal biases or prejudices clouding assessments

Before we discuss how we can give feedback constructively, let's listen in on the following feedback conversation.

Managerial Anecdote

Yee Ling, a young logistics specialist, works for Peter, the supply chain director of a consumer electronics company based in Shanghai. Peter is an American expatriate. Three months ago, he invited Yee Ling to join a company-wide task force that he personally chairs. He has become rather disappointed as Yee Ling has not contributed at all in the four meetings that have been convened. In his mind, she clearly has no interest in the proceedings. In his usual forthright way, Peter decides to call Yee Ling into his office to give her some feedback.

Peter: *I would like to provide you some feedback about your participation in the company-wide task force.*

Yee Ling: *Sure, what's your feedback?*

Peter: *I now have second thoughts about whether I did the right thing in inviting you to join me in the task force. My aim was to provide you a chance to observe me in managing such a large cross-functional team. I was hoping that as you're new to our company this will hasten your assimilation and expose you to other people in the company. But apparently, you have no interest in the discussions. You are always silent in all the discussions.*

Yee Ling: *Boss, I'm sorry that you think that way...I am learning a lot and I assure you that I'm very interested.*

Peter: *It sure doesn't seem that way to me. Of the seven people present, you're the only one who has contributed nothing so far. So do you really want to remain in the team?*

Yee Ling: *Yes, boss. I definitely want to stay on as it helps me a lot to observe how you and the other experienced people work together. I will contribute more from now onwards.*

If you were Yee Ling, what is the impact of this conversation on you? Chances are the encounter has unsettled you. Peter's remarks are too direct and insensitive. He has already made up his mind that you aren't interested. Visibly unhappy, he wants you to buck up or leave.

You feel rather hurt as well. What a judgmental boss! He doesn't even ask why you have been quiet in the last few sessions and simply jumps to conclusions based on his own assumptions. You're the newest kid in the block and the youngest and most inexperienced among all the members. Everyone else is a manager except you. In such a setting, you gather it is better for you to listen and pick up more before you say anything. But apparently, the boss doesn't see things that way. You'd better start speaking up, even if there isn't much to say.

The bottom line here is that instead of being constructive and helping Yee Ling, Peter has provoked defensiveness. She will trust him less and will be more wary. There is little likelihood that there will be any real benefit from this feedback.

A FEEDBACK FRAMEWORK THAT WORKS

Here are five steps for creating feedback conversations that will be well-received and lead to positive actions. In other words, good feedback is actionable.

Step 1: Adopt an open mindset

When you give feedback, it is because you have certain observations about what has taken place. This may then lead you to interpret these events in a certain way. It is important to know that your interpretation is only one plausible way of viewing things. They may be other factors that you aren't aware of. Hence, it is advisable to stay open-minded and refrain from passing judgment.

Peter's approach is a case in point. He sees Yee Ling's silence as evidence of lack of interest and quickly becomes disappointed. On the contrary, she is excited and honoured to be in the task force. Being a young Chinese girl in the midst of more senior and experienced colleagues, she is hesitant to speak out of turns.

Step 2: Make feedback a gift

When feedback is framed as a means to reach a specific organizational goal, it becomes an opportunity rather than a problem. For instance, it becomes an opportunity to develop people, improve customer service, or improve market share. When people see feedback as an investment in their development or a means to help them become more successful, it is now viewed as a gift.

Step 3: Be specific and focus on behaviour

Before you deliver feedback, ask yourself whether you have concrete evidence that may support your feedback. Make sure you do. Otherwise, when you conduct the conversation, it may even come across as half-baked and even frivolous. Do not base your feedback on rumours and hearsay.

The Centre for Creative Leadership (CCL) has a feedback model that I have found useful. Called SBI (Situation Behaviour Impact), there are three components as follows:

Situation:	The setting or event that comprises the context for the behaviour to occur.
Example:	*"During the task force meetings in the last four months..."*

Behaviour:	Description of the behaviour observed.
Example:	*"I noticed that you did not share your opinions with the rest of us."*

Impact:	Tell the person how her behaviour is affecting you or the group.
Example:	*"I have a sense that perhaps these meetings aren't as useful for you as I had hoped."*

It is important to note that we should focus specifically on behaviour and not say anything about the person's character or attitude. You may say, "I have a sense that these meetings aren't as useful for you as I had hoped." But it is presumptuous to say, "You have no interest in the discussions."

Avoid making personal remarks or judging the person as in "... apparently, you have no interest in the discussions." Once you do that, the other party will get defensive, and the conversation will go south.

Step 4: Check for response
To keep the conversation open and on even keel, pause a little to let the other party take in your feedback. Then ask some questions to solicit his or her reaction.

> Examples: *"How useful is it for you so far in participating in the task force meetings?"*
> *"What do you think is the best way for you to learn and contribute at the meetings?"*

Questions like these are open-ended and non-judgmental. By being patient and willing to listen, you are making the conversation safe for the other party.

Yee Ling may respond as follows: *"It's actually very useful for me. I'm learning a lot. I'm sorry that I've been quiet... As I'm still new and inexperienced, I was afraid of saying the wrong things."*

Through her response, you may then realize that she's probably still feeling uncomfortable in speaking up. In Asia, people tend to be less forthcoming in sharing their views in the presence of their seniors and elders.

Step 5: Follow-through
Don't stop here. The next step after listening and understanding is to encourage actions to help your subordinate improve. You may

empathize with her about being uncomfortable in speaking up as she is still new. Do assure her that the beginner's view may provide a refreshingly different perspective. And this is a good environment to learn how to influence others.

In fact, a good feedback session may be a segue for a subsequent coaching conversation. Ask, "How will you act differently in our next meeting? How can I support you?"

Both of you may agree that in future meetings, you may cue her by asking for her viewpoints. Once invited, she may be more open in contributing. In the weeks ahead, you may have a brief chat with her to discuss her progress. Do remember to compliment her for her effort. With your encouragement, she will find her voice before long.

APPLYING THE FEEDBACK FRAMEWORK

Review the five-step approach and be familiar with it. Before giving feedback, spend some time going through each of the five steps and mentally rehearsing what you will say. You may even consider role-playing with a trusted colleague.

Feedback that is useful needs to be delivered in a timely fashion. Don't wait too long to either compliment someone for a piece of work or help him make a much needed improvement. Do it when the event is still fresh in the mind. There is a caveat though. If you or the other party are feeling upset, then it's best to wait for a day or two to regain a proper perspective before having the conversation.

GIVING FEEDBACK ON THE FLY[2]

The five-step approach is useful in a one-one-one conversation with co-workers. When the session is conducted in privacy, there is more room for candour and clarification. There will, however, be occasions when you need to give feedback on the fly, so to speak. On such occasions, you have to do it less formally and may not have the time nor the privacy to adopt the five-step approach.

For instance, you are in a meeting during which a subordinate or a colleague has just presented a plan. You do have some ideas that may enhance his proposal. How should you proceed? I recommend a two-step approach as follows:

Step 1: Acknowledge the merits of what you have just heard, i.e. What Went Well (WWW).

Step 2: Provide suggestions for his consideration i.e. Even Better If (EBI)

For instance, you may say: "If we put ourselves in the shoes of our client, the merits of this proposal are as follows: (a)... (b)... and (c)... Perhaps, our chances of winning this bid may be even better if you include an option for..."

Between Steps 1 and 2, many of us have an instinctive urge to insert the word "but". Doing so gives an unmistakable feeling that what is said in Step 1 is insincere. So let's avoid it. If you need to use a conjunction, try "and". It connects Steps 1 and 2 more constructively and seamlessly.

TYPES OF FEEDBACK

Positive

This applies to situations where someone has performed something very well and you wish to acknowledge him for it. It will be much more genuine and impactful if you adopt the SBI approach. Remember to provide concrete examples of what you appreciate. Managers should make the effort to show appreciation a little more often. In Asia and Europe, there is a tendency to withhold praises.

Constructive

This is for the purpose of helping the other party make improvement. As managers, we definitely need to do this more. Our people want it. Peter's feedback would have been very useful for Yee Ling if he had done it the proper way.

Negative

It is for the purpose of pointing out an extreme form of behaviour that is completely unacceptable. Prior to this, the manager will have tried to provide constructive feedback. Now many attempts later, it has reached a make-or-break juncture. It's time for a difficult conversation.

HAVING A DIFFICULT CONVERSATION

Not all constructive feedback discussions will turn out well. While most people will appreciate your feedback, there will be some who may become emotional and defensive.

When the other party becomes upset, it is best to pause and remain calm. If necessary, suggest that the discussion be adjourned to another date. Let him cool down a little. Then, reconvene the session. By that time, that person may have reflected on what you have said and may be more receptive

There may also be cases, however, where the subordinate may ignore the feedback and take no actions to improve. You will see this kind of behaviour in recalcitrant employees who have been allowed to have things their way for far too long by other bosses. Ironically, some star employees may just be as resistant to constructive feedback. In their eyes, they can do no wrong. What then do you do?

Remember: You get what you tolerate.

Stay composed and schedule a few more follow-up sessions. But there must come a time when you will need to lay out the cold, hard facts that failure to respond to the feedback will lead to serious consequences. For instance, you may have someone who performs well but is habitually abusive and foul-mouthed. This is when you exercise the hard power that you possess as a manager. It is useful to link his behaviour back to the corporate values.

Before you reach this point, talk to your boss and consult with HR (Human Resources). Then be courageous. Deliver the tough message. Effective managers do not shirk from taking unpopular but necessary measures that are for the good of the organization.

You may put it this way, for instance: "We have discussed on many occasions your habit of abusing colleagues and using foul language. This is a serious violation of our core value of treating colleagues with human sensitivity. Despite our conversations, I have seen no improvement on your part. I'll be left with no choice but to terminate your employment contract with us if there is another instance of this kind of behaviour from you."

FEEDBACK AND PERFORMANCE APPRAISALS

Good managers schedule regular coaching sessions one-on-one with their reports. Such sessions serve the purpose of facilitating their development. They will also provide the context for providing feedback regularly. Such a practice will take the sting out of the dreaded annual performance review.

There will therefore be no surprises when it's time for the yearly performance appraisal. What needs to be discussed and improved has already been highlighted, agreed and worked on. Done this way, a learning partnership between the boss and the subordinate emerges. Performance appraisal thus morphs from an annual event to a sincere, ongoing developmental dialogue.

- Employees will benefit immensely through receiving regular feedback from their bosses on their performance.

- Most managers find it difficult to provide feedback. The five-step feedback framework will help you to make feedback more objective and actionable.

Q1: When was the last time you gave feedback to one of your subordinates? How well was it done?

Q2: Try using the feedback framework in your next coaching conversations with your people.

13 ASKING FOR FEEDBACK

WHY MANAGERS NEED FEEDBACK

Managers who provide constructive feedback to their subordinates are adding immense value to their organization. Likewise, they will also benefit greatly if they ask for and receive feedback for themselves. These are some key benefits:

- Managers need to walk the talk. Since they recognize that providing feedback to subordinates is a vital part of their responsibilities, they need to set an example of being willing to accept feedback from others.
- Feedback will help managers discover others' perspective of how they are behaving. It will provide insights on blind spots. It is also a gift from others.
- Managers have bosses too. And bosses will at the end of the year deliver that mandatory annual performance review. By asking for feedback regularly from others, including bosses, they will help to make the annual review with the bosses less stressful.
- If managers develop a habit of being open to feedback and leverage it to improve themselves, it will set the stage for a learning culture. This will augur well for the future of the company.

ASK AND YOU MAY NOT RECEIVE

While giving feedback is fraught with challenges, asking for feedback is even more difficult. These are common issues encountered:

- Managers themselves are very uncomfortable asking for feedback. Many fear being vulnerable. Once we become the boss, there is an image that we need to uphold: that of someone who is capable and self-confident. If we ask for feedback and it turns out to be critical of us or our performance, then we will lose face or feel embarrassed.

- Subordinates are generally fearful of appearing to criticize their bosses. In the Western culture, people are more forthcoming in providing input if asked for by their bosses. Nonetheless, even they will couch or pad their words. It takes a very brave, perhaps foolhardy soul, to openly speak what is in her mind about her boss. In Asia, generally, few people will give real and genuine feedback. It could be the career equivalent of committing *hara-kiri*—or self-destruction.

> Please be candid about how good a boss you think I am!

> But will you fire me if I speak the truth?

ASK FOR FEEDFORWARD INSTEAD OF FEEDBACK

Let's watch a scenario involving a manager Sarah who is keen to seek feedback from her subordinates. She is new to her role and her teammates do not know her well. She has just done a rehearsal of a presentation with her team. This is in preparation for a senior management meeting to be held the following week.

Managerial Anecdote

After completing the 20-minute presentation with a set of Powerpoint slides, Sarah says, "Please give me some feedback. What are the areas that I have not done well and must be improved by next week?"

This is met with silence. Nobody says anything for what seems like forever—three minutes. Finally, one person, Arun, speaks up, "I think it is very informative. It really gives a complete picture about what we have done as a team."

Sarah thanks Arun and asks whether the others have anything else to add. They all say no. She then adjourns the meeting.

That evening, Sarah calls one of her friends for advice. This friend is an experienced senior manager in another company. She has a reputation of being able to engage co-workers very effectively. People who work with her trust and respect her.

This is what the friend suggests: "Sarah, before people will give you any feedback they need to be comfortable with you. And if you're the boss, it's a little trickier. You have joined the company for less than a month. This makes you an unknown to them.

Instead of asking for feedback, I think that a better and more effective approach is to ask for feedforward. Feedback focuses on the past and it seeks information on what you have not done well. Put yourself in the shoes of your subordinates. How comfortable will they be to point out shortcomings in your presentation?"

Sarah listens intently. Then she says, "I see your point. Now I know why they didn't say much. But I still need to know what needs to be improved. Better find out now than commit the mistakes in the presence of the big bosses."

"You're right, Sarah," the friend replies. "But asking for feedback is not the way to go. Depersonalize it by asking for feedforward. While feedback focuses on the past, feedforward, as the word implies, talks about the future. Say this to them instead,

"As you are aware, we'll do this presentation to senior management next week. How can we improve our presentation in order for us to secure approval for our project?"

The following day, Sarah invites her team for a chat again. She then asks for feedforward. Her people are indeed more willing to speak up. She is definitely pleased with the insightful input provided. Now, she feels that her team is with her for the upcoming presentation.

WHY PEOPLE WILL RESPOND TO REQUESTS FOR FEEDFORWARD[1]

I owe a debt of gratitude to Marshall Goldsmith who first taught me this concept. Most people—subordinates, peers and bosses— are uncomfortable about giving feedback. We have discussed this at length in the previous chapter. So why force the issue? It's like trying to squeeze blood from stones.

Help yourself by making it easier for them. Don't ask them to tell you what you have done poorly. That's the past. Ask them instead to help you to perform better in the future. That's what feedforward is about: the future. Try this and you will be amazed how much more forthcoming they will become.

Here are two examples:

1. If you have just completed a piece of work and would like to improve it further, ask, "What can I do differently to get even better results the next time?"

2. If you would like to have candid input about yourself, ask "What are one or two things that will help me become even more effective?"

If, despite having asked for feedforward, people still aren't willing to speak up, it may be that there is still a high level of discomfort. Recently, I was speaking to a number of senior Asian leaders in the government service. They were mostly of one voice on the topic of providing input to their bosses. The preferred approach is to do it behind the scene and one-on-one. Therefore, if you sense that you still aren't getting what you need, invite your subordinates for a private chat. The onus is on you to consider ways to lighten up the working atmosphere so that people feel safe to speak up.

- Just as giving feedback to your subordinates will aid their development, receiving feedback will do the same for you as a manager.

- People are generally reluctant to give feedback to bosses as it may be construed as a form of criticism. Try asking for feedforward. They may become more forthcoming.

Q1: How will you respond if your boss asks you for feedback? What if she asks for feedforward instead?

Q2: Try asking for feedforward at work. Evaluate how useful, candid and actionable the input that you receive is.

PART FOUR
Managing Teams

2. Managing Team Members	3. Managing Teams
1. Managing Yourself	
4. Managing Key Relationships	5. Becoming A More Complete Leader

*"The leaders who work most effectively, it seems to me,
never say "I". And that's not because they trained
themselves not to say "I". They don't think "I".
They think "we"; they think "team." They understand their job
to be to make the team function. They accept responsibility
and don't sidestep it, but "we" gets the credit. That is
what creates trust, what enables you to get the task done."*
—Peter Drucker

14 BECOMING A TEAM LEADER

WHY HAVE TEAMS?

The first thing you will notice when you become a manager is that you are now responsible for working with various people to collectively achieve certain goals. Your relationship with these people will take either of the following forms: (a) they report directly to you, or (b) they are co-workers, over whom you have no direct authority and whose support you will nonetheless need. Another dimension that is increasingly common now is that, whether it is (a) or (b), these people may be located in different countries from you. In other words, the team may be virtual.

As a manager, you will spend a considerable amount of your time in meetings or in a team setting, perhaps 30 to 90 percent. This is by any standards a considerable investment of your time and energy. You will quickly realize that to become effective as a manager, you need to play the team game successfully.

The importance of your ability to lead and influence teams can't be overestimated. This is more challenging and complex than one-on-one leadership. Upon this your overall success as a first-time manager will be determined. Subsequently, it will define whether you will continue to ascend up the corporate ladder.

These are the key reasons why teams are now the central vehicle for getting work done:

- A team of people can achieve much more, and faster than individual workers working separately;
- Teams are better able to tackle complex problems than traditional hierarchical structures;
- In a team environment, the collective expertise and richness of diverse perspectives provide a competitive advantage;
- In the globalized workplace with personnel geographically dispersed, business objectives can only be achieved by linking such people into a virtual network.

WHY TEAMS FAIL[1]

Unfortunately, getting a group of people together and turning them into a real high-performing team is a tough act to do. We all have experienced manifestations of dysfunctional teams. For instance, after countless team meetings, people leave feeling that no resolution has been reached. Another common situation is that of a group of busy and responsible people assembling regularly to work on important matters. Yet, for some inexplicable reasons, the participants skim the surface in their discussions, skirt the real issues and then quickly agree on actions that none in particular feels accountable for. In other words, it has been a complete waste of everybody's time.

These are six top reasons why teams fail to live up to their expectations:

- Lack of team leadership;
- It is not a real team; just what you might refer to as a collection of individuals;
- Lack of trust;
- No clear and compelling purpose;
- No commitment and accountability to a common purpose;
- Lack of complementary knowledge, skills and experience.

I would like to share a real-life case of a group of individuals who pretended that they were a team.

Managerial Anecdote

Patrick had recently been appointed as General Manager of a business unit in an ASEAN country. After about two months, he became concerned that he wasn't getting much value from his senior management meetings. He wanted an outside perspective on what was happening. I was invited by him to sit in at one of his weekly management meetings.

It was a well-planned meeting with an agenda organized by key functions such as sales, marketing, finance, manufacturing, supply chain, HR, etc. What I saw was a lot of Patrick speaking and little real exchange amongst his people. As the GM went through the agenda, he would direct his attention to those members of his management team whose functions were being discussed. At the end of the dialogue, some follow-up action would apparently be "agreed."

And so it went for all agenda items, with different members taking turns to have a dialogue with him. As this was going on, I scanned the room. The senior managers were waiting quietly and patiently for their respective items to appear. At one stage, one manager had a point to raise whilst a dialogue was going on between Patrick and another manager. He tried to speak up but his words fell flat. Patrick did not even acknowledge what he had said.

When the meeting ended, Patrick invited me to share my observations with him in his office.

In our debrief, I said that from watching the group dynamics, the attendees weren't a team but a collection of individuals. Although they all reported to Patrick, it wasn't clear what other common grounds existed. To be sure, each manager as head of his respective function, knew what his KPIs and responsibilities were. But he assumed that the meeting was mainly for reporting on work matters. Teams, however, can be leveraged for the purpose of collaboration to achieve something larger. If it was for the latter, no one knew what that larger thing was. Patrick had never explained that to them, it seemed.

I then shared with Patrick the concept of wearing two hats. As all his managers were members of the company's senior leadership team, each individual therefore had to wear two hats. Their first hat was to lead their respective functions in the best possible way. Their second hat was that of responsibility for the business. As senior leaders, they had an overarching responsibility to collaborate with each other to steer the company to attain its overall vision. Each time the GM convened a management meeting, it should be to focus on moving the company towards its overall goals and vision. That would be the best use of the senior leadership's time and resources. Members should attend the meeting wearing their second hat. Alas, because neither Patrick nor his managers understood this concept, the meetings devolved into a reporting session on functional matters. They all had their first hat on throughout.

In terms of team leadership, Patrick's style of running the meeting was that of an autocrat sitting at the head of the table. Through his body language and mannerisms, he was telling all that this was a meeting for each manager to make a progress report on his area of responsibility. The preferred vehicle would be a dialogue between him and the respective manager. By not openly encouraging cross exchanges, he was unwittingly yet effectively reinforcing a silo mindset among the managers.

Trust was definitely missing. The members were still wary of the new GM. Among themselves, as I found out later, they had an unspoken agreement that if there were common issues between them, they would resolve these outside the meetings. Bringing them up in the GM's presence would only complicate matters. Hence, there was next to no constructive conflict. If any "agreement" was reached, nobody felt any sense of accountability.

WHAT IS A TEAM?

There is a tendency to use the word "team" very loosely. Some people think that every time a number of people come together, they have a team. That's really not true. For the purpose of our discussion, let's differentiate between "working groups" and "teams."

A working group consists of a number of people who come together on an ad hoc basis to address certain tasks such as providing information for a report to be prepared, or to tackle a customer complaint. People in a working group can work independently and contribute to the tasks on hand.

A team consists of a small number of people with a common

purpose and complementary skills. They subscribe to a certain approach and will hold each other mutually accountable in the fulfilment of their common goals. Members need to work interdependently to be successful.

There is a need for managers to recognize that having a team is not the solution to everything. There will be situations when it will be more productive for individuals to work alone. There will also be situations when teamwork is the only way to tackle a certain challenge. Managers therefore need to balance between individual autonomy and collective effort.

We'll discuss how a team can be formed and developed in the following chapter.

THE CHALLENGES OF TEAM LEADERSHIP

In Part Two, we spent a considerable amount of time discussing how to lead and manage individuals. When you start to lead a team, a higher level of leadership is required.

These are some key prerequisites:

1. Realize that in order for the team to achieve its common goals, you will need synergy and collaboration. Unlike working groups, whose performance depends on individual contribution, effective teams will have an impact that is beyond the sum of individual parts. This is the concept of wearing two hats. While each member has her own individual responsibilities, she also has team responsibilities. Only through working interdependently will the overall team vision be attainable.

2. As a team leader, you are a key determinant of your team's success or failure. You will need to be competent in facilitating, coaching and guiding your members, thereby creating the right environment for teamwork to take root and flourish.

3. While performing (2), the team leader needs to recognize that he does not have all the answers. He therefore strives

to strike a critical balance between directing the team and letting the members step up to a shared leadership.

4. For high-performance to be attained, the team leader needs to be willing to share decision-making and control with the members. An unwillingness to do so will stifle the growth of the team. Doing so will require taking risks and making . good judgment calls. Thus, be emotionally and mentally prepared to make some mistakes.

5. For a team to be truly effective, it has to take on its own character like any social group does. The right environment must be created to engender mutual trust and a sense of group identity, i.e. members are fully engaged with each other emotionally.

• Leading a team is much more complex than leading individuals.

• Teams are the central vehicle for getting complex work done. With an effective and cohesive team, more can be achieved at a faster pace than when individuals work alone.

Q1: In the anecdote, what could Patrick have done differently to make his meetings more interactive and productive?

Q2: In your own work environment, how much work is done through individuals working independently? How much is done through teamwork? What will you do differently to raise productivity?

15 FORMING AND DEVELOPING YOUR TEAM

EIGHT CONDITIONS FOR SUCCESSFUL TEAMWORK

For teams to be successful, these eight conditions must exist:
1. Effective team leadership
2. A clear and compelling vision
3. Members are fully committed to the vision
4. Members are aligned with one another
5. Complementary competencies
6. Every member contributes, every member benefits
7. Climate of trust, pride and motivation
8. Training and development

FIVE STAGES OF TEAM DEVELOPMENT[1]

Like individuals, teams will go through a series of developmental stages as they evolve. In general, there are essentially five stages of team development: orientation, dissatisfaction, integration, performance and termination. In the last few decades, various researchers such as Tuckman and Lacoursiere have done studies on the life cycle of groups. The latter in particular views groups as living organisms. They grow and are subjected to stresses and will either mature or degenerate as a result of these stresses.

It is necessary for team leaders to understand these developmental stages. At each stage the team will exhibit certain characteristics and will have specific needs. By understanding what these are, managers will be better equipped to facilitate the building and development of a cohesive and effective team. Basically, team leaders need to attend to two categories of processes: **task-related**—those that define what each member should be doing; and **socio-emotional**—those that bring about greater trust and cohesion.

Stage 1: Orientation

When people come together to join a team for the first time, there is usually a lot of excitement and anticipation. At the same time, there will be anxiety and uncertainty. In many cases, they may not know who the other members are. Though they may know who the team leader is, it may only be by name and reputation. Also, they are unclear what the team goals and objectives are, and especially what their individual roles and responsibilities will be. Typically, these are the ways people will behave:

- Polite, cautious, curious;
- Participation is uneven; some will speak more than others;
- Sizing up the team leader;
- Members wishing to know their place in the team; and
- Members looking to the team leader to provide clarity and direction.

While morale may be high, productivity is low at this stage.

How managers should facilitate: At this stage, the team leader needs to provide direction and clarity and win the trust of the members. His struggle will be to balance between providing direction, purpose and structure and not coming across to his members as someone who seems to be a know-it-all. He will feel less conflicted by realizing that at the point in time, the members' desire for direction and purpose will far outweigh their needs to have greater say and participation. These are the key steps:

- Define common purpose and goal;
- Discuss and affirm team composition to ensure complementary competencies;
- Show the way by discussing roadmap towards objectives;
- Start the trust-building process by introducing himself and inviting all others to do the same. Create an atmosphere of inclusiveness so that every member can find his own place in the team;

- Invite members to define and endorse ground rules;
- Collectively define roles, responsibilities and accountabilities of every member including his own.

Stage 2: Dissatisfaction

At this stage, the members have been working with each other for a short while. Difficulties are likely to have surfaced either in terms of getting tasks accomplished or securing necessary resources. Some members may also find that not everyone on the team is aligned in terms of common goals. Sub-groups may be forming. Interpersonal conflicts may also have arisen. As gaps are appearing between initial expectations and reality, team members may be getting frustrated with their relationship with the team leader. In an Asian environment, members are unlikely to openly challenge the team leader though. Both morale and productivity continue to dip.

How managers should facilitate: In Chapter 5 we discussed the importance of EQ in interacting with others. As a team leader, this will become even more crucial. Through his empathy, the team leader will now sense that his members are feeling a little disillusioned. The team leader will need to continue to win the confidence of the members by clarifying directions. At the same time, he will need to draw his people out to share their thoughts and to collectively focus on solutions. Much of the conflict may be due to different working styles or even cultural differences. It may be necessary to provide training to the team to understand, appreciate and manage diversity. There will also be a need to invest in team-building activities to engender greater mutual trust. These are the key steps:
- Reaffirm overall purpose and goal;
- Ask for input on issues that have arisen and work collectively to resolve them;
- Listen and make room for differing opinions to be voiced;
- Provide training and invest in team-building activities;

- Invite members to discuss conflicts openly. In Asia, members tend to be wary about airing conflicts "publicly". Managers may have to play by ear, tailor their approaches to the different personalities of team members, and work in smaller groups to bring about resolution;
- Encourage members to work interdependently; and
- Objectively and firmly address instances of non-compliance to ground rules.

Stage 3: Integration
Team members are starting to become more comfortable working with each other. There is greater clarity in what each member should be doing and progress is becoming visible. People are more comfortable and there is rising confidence and pride as tasks are getting accomplished. Having just transitioned from the rather difficult dissatisfaction stage, the relationship is still a little fragile. There will be some members who still aren't fully on-board and are sitting on the sideline. Morale and productivity are improving.

How managers should facilitate: At this stage, the basic team processes are in place. Members probably know what they all have to do individually and collectively. The key challenge now is to engender that sense of social bonding and camaraderie so that members grow into a cohesive and effective team. This can only happen when there is strong mutual trust and members are at the same emotional wavelength with each other.

These are some key steps:
- Provide a safe environment for members to provide constructive feedback to each other. A real indicator of progress is the ability to openly discuss individual strengths and areas for development;
- Continue to identify and resolve interpersonal conflicts;
- Encourage collaboration and interdependency;
- Invite members to share leadership of the team;

- Invite members to take greater ownership for identifying and resolving obstacles. Be open to reviewing ground rules, roles and responsibilities;
- Celebrate success;
- Ensure that the team is kept abreast of external development through training and development.

Stage 4: Performance

The team is now maturing. Productivity and morale are high. Members are proud of being part of the team and there is a sense of pride. Activities are progressing very well and there is collaboration throughout. Team members openly communicate with each other and hold each other to high standards. There is a sense of shared leadership with members proactively addressing challenges as they arise. The energy level is high and there is a frequent expression of humour.

How managers should facilitate: With the team humming to the same upbeat tune, the manager knows that the most difficult part of developing his team is behind. Now is the time to empower and encourage shared leadership so that the team can reach their higher potential.

These are the key steps he can take:
- Acknowledge and celebrate successes;
- Set new challenges and higher standards;
- Encourage greater autonomy within agreed boundaries;
- Focus on developing members for higher responsibilities;
- Send members for professional conferences and training programmes; and
- Act more as a coach than as a manager.

Stage 5: Termination

All teams will come to an end at some point in time. For ongoing teams, this is not really a termination but a temporary lull as a goal is achieved or a milestone is reached. At this stage, it will be useful for the team to celebrate its success and recharge itself. The team leader will need to re-energize and reorganize the team for the next set of challenges.

For a task force, this could really be an ending point as the objectives have been attained and there is no need for it to continue. There will inevitably be some sadness tinged with pride on what has been accomplished. The team leader and other senior people can send the members off to combat other challenges by expressing appreciation for a project well done.

CREATING A HIGH-PERFORMING TEAM

Managers around the world and at all levels in the organization generally aren't getting as much out of teams as they should. There are two main reasons: (a) a lack of understanding of the eight conditions for effective teamwork and (b) the team leader and the members do not go through the stages of team development. In brief, teams don't work because the people never really become a real team.

The case of the GM, Patrick, is quite typical. He had the notion that all he had to do was to convene regular business reviews to get the most out of his team. As you have seen, he only succeeded in driving his people deep into their own silos.

As managers progress further up the hierarchy, the challenges of creating effective teams become compounded by higher complexities and ambiguities. And, without high-performing teams, organizations will lose out in terms of competitiveness and nimbleness.

The best time to acquire the basics of leading teams is when you are a first-time manager. Teams at this level are simpler in composition and interpersonal relations are easier to manage. We'll now elaborate on the eight conditions for effective teamwork.

1. Effective team leadership

The team leader has heavy responsibilities to shoulder. He is leader, manager, coach, facilitator and cheer leader bundled into one. He will be the first to bring a bunch of co-workers together, and over time and with much hard work, create the conditions and motivation for them to pool their talents and energies in the service of a larger team vision. This is the captain of the soccer team whom we talked about in Chapter 1.

2. A clear and compelling vision
What do you want to accomplish out of the team that can't be done by the members working alone? How exciting will this goal be for yourself and the members?

3. Members are fully committed to the vision
When you gather the members for your first meeting, these are some questions in their minds as they listen to you articulating the vision: Does this excite me? What's in it for me (WIIFM). Why will working as a team help me to meet or exceed my KPIs? What exactly is the overall goal for the team?

4. Members are aligned with one another
Why will members want to work with each other? After all, working independently is far more efficient and less aggravating. This is the concept of wearing two hats.

5. Complementary competencies
Members need to be convinced that everyone in the team will bring some talent or resources that others may need but may not possess. This addresses the fifth condition. They need to work interdependently to meet the overall goals.

6. Every member contributes, every member benefits
Working in a team is hard work and time-consuming. When members contribute, how will they benefit from it? Is there some recognition from you? Do they acquire new skills? Do they get exposure to senior management?

7. Climate of trust, pride and motivation

This is the socio-emotional aspect of teamwork. We have discussed the importance of trust at various places throughout this book. Invest time and effort in creating a climate that people want to work in.

8. Training and development

Teams don't click on their own. They need to be nurtured. It's your job as the team leader to provide the appropriate training to help it move from one stage to the next. Your learning and development organization will be a good resource for you.

And for the team manager, please remember that each team is unique and so is its context. The best team leader, like the soccer captain in Chapter 1, is always adapting and improvising constantly as the game evolves.

MANAGING VIRTUAL TEAMS[2]

It is becoming increasingly common for companies to organize business activities which require team members to be based in dispersed geographic locations. Generally, these team members may come from different cultural backgrounds and speak different languages. They may also not report to the team leader as they may come from different departments. This is the matrix structure that is becoming very common.

Not surprisingly, collaboration becomes a much greater challenge as distance amplifies difficulties in communication and coordination. As the virtual team members may not get to meet in person, it definitely makes it harder to establish rapport and mutual trust. As we have discussed earlier, without trust and alignment to a common vision, there will be a greater potential for conflict. Yet another issue is the need to negotiate multiple time zones to set up teleconferences or web meetings.

Though virtual teams face more difficulties in working together than teams that are co-located, it is still possible to help them realize their full potential. The prerequisites are still that there must be sufficient effort and attention devoted to the two key processes of team-building: task-related and socio-emotional.

If you are managing a virtual team for the first time, here are a few lessons culled from organizations that have experiences with virtual teams.

1. Learn how to run a conventional co-located team successfully
The principles of forming and developing an effective virtual team are the same as those for traditional face-to-face teams. Make sure that you know what they are and have applied them successfully in leading a conventional team before you attempt to lead a virtual team.

2. Provide for face-to-face meetings
When people are able to meet each other face-to-face, they are able to put a face to a name. This can work wonders for key social processes. It will encourage informal communication, friendship, team cohesion and identification. If you are embarking on a project, kicking off the project face-to-face is a good chance to bring everyone together. This is when you may initiate the task-related processes (defining team purpose, roles and responsibilities, roadmap, etc.) and socio-emotional processes (trust-building, getting to know each other, understanding and appreciating diversity, etc.).

3. Use technology to enhance collaboration
Explore, test and leverage high-tech tools that can raise productivity and interactivity. These include web conferences where colleagues can see one another, voting tools for anonymous feedback, collaborative online presentation capability, raising hand virtually to ask questions or to make a point, etc.

4. Ensure virtual meetings are interactive
If there is a need to provide a lot of information to the participants,

do not have a teleconference. Send an email ahead of time with the necessary attachments. Or do a webcast.

Keep your virtual meetings action-packed with the agenda clearly defined ahead of time. Reporting of progress should be done concisely. If there are issues that involve certain members of the team but not the rest, schedule a separate session to address them.

5. Adopt an equal inconvenience approach
Alternate meeting times so that people in different time zones share the inconvenience of either staying up very late at night or waking up very early for the meetings. Asia-based participants frequently find themselves working a 14-hour shift when calls are scheduled at 9 p.m. or 10 p.m. because it is 8 a.m. or 9 a.m. in the United States and 3 p.m. in Europe. Many of them accept this arrangement without qualms in the interest of accommodating team members in other parts of the hemisphere. I strongly suggest that they raise this matter for discussion and request for meeting times to be alternated.

6. Emphasize collaboration and relationship building
Encourage team members to work closely with one another on an ongoing basis through the phone, email or video conferences. If they encounter issues with each other, call each other up and discuss directly. As the team leader, watch for signs of conflict and intervene if necessary.

- You may not need teams for every situation. Sometimes, it is more productive for individuals to work independently.

- To create a high-performing team, the team leader needs to invest time and effort to move it from one stage to the next.

Q1: How effective is your own team currently?

Q2: What will you do to form and develop your team?

16 MANAGING TEAM DYNAMICS

WHAT ARE TEAM DYNAMICS?

When people work together in a team environment, there are unseen forces at work which will impact the way they behave, react and perform. Such forces give rise to team dynamics. They may include individual behavioural styles, team roles, office layout, organizational culture, office politics, etc. In this chapter, we'll discuss individual behavioural styles and team roles.

Team members need to be trained to understand, appreciate and manage team dynamics. They are a double-edged sword. Handled well, they will be sources of strengths and creativity. If misunderstood and poorly managed, there will be endless conflict and tension. Working in a team may become a nightmare.

INDIVIDUAL BEHAVIOURAL STYLES

People who work together quickly realize that each person has her own unique style of behaving, communicating and operating. When faced with a particular situation, someone of a particular style will consistently behave in a certain way. In responding to the same situation, people of other styles will however behave differently.

For instance, a team is faced with a difficult task that needs to be completed very quickly and yet information for decision-making is inadequate. Some members will become quiet and cautious and will want to investigate the task further before committing to a course of action. In contrast, there will also be some others who are quite ready to act based on whatever data and information are available. How do you think these two groups of people will view each other?

To the first group, the second group is hasty and is willing to sacrifice quality and thoroughness for speed. To the second group, the first group is dragging its feet and unable to see the big picture.

While such differences will enrich the environment through a diversity of perspectives and approaches, the downside is that they may lead to conflict and clashes. When a working relationship is derailed, all hopes of teamwork will be dashed.

For team members to work effectively with each other, they will need an understanding of the different styles of interaction that their co-workers will exhibit. Through this understanding, what may initially appear to be a major misalignment in values and priorities will now be seen more constructively.

There are various models, such as the MBTI and the DISC,[1] that will help to explain the different behavioural styles. Both are easy to understand and apply. Our discussion will be based on the DISC, which is the simpler of the two models.

The DISC-theory was derived from studies conducted by early 20th century behavioural scientists. In diagram 16.1, you will notice that there two scales: (a) Results- vs People-Orientation and (b) Details vs Big-picture. Their studies identify four behavioural styles which are defined by the four quadrants as follows: D (Dominant) style; I (Influencing) style; S (Steady) style; C (Compliant) style. Refer to Table 16.1 on the facing page for the characteristics of each style.

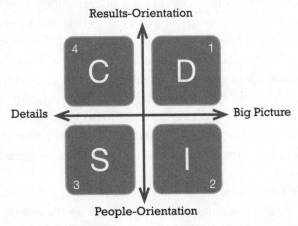

Diagram 16.1: The DISC Profile

Table 16.1: Characteristics of each DISC style

	STRENGTHS	WEAKNESSES	UNDER PRESSURE	FEAR
D	• Results-oriented • Decisive • Tough • Confident • Fast-paced • Competitive • Visionary	• Bossy • Impatient • Poor listener • Overbearing • Abrasive • Gloss over details	• Ignore feelings of others	• Loss of control
I	• Outgoing • Sociable • Likeable • Influential • Creative • Engaging • Energetic	• Excitable • Careless • Not detailed • More concerned about talking than delivering	• Disorganized	• Social rejection
S	• Steady • Patient • Empathetic • Calm • People-oriented • Trustworthy • Good mediator	• Too accommodating • Risk-averse • Prefers status quo • Not sufficiently hard-nosed	• Overly-sympathetic	• Loss of stability
C	• Analytical • Logical • Precise • Careful • Conform to rules	• Unemotional • Bogged down by details	• Inflexible	• Criticism of their work

UNDERSTANDING STYLE DIFFERENCES

First, it is necessary to note that in the DISC model, no single style is better or worse than the others. They all have strengths and weaknesses. Successful people come in all the different styles.

By understanding the various styles, we can better predict how people will respond to external stimuli. It is a tool for recognizing and observing behaviours but not for analyzing an individual's whole personality. Such insights enable us to understand ourselves and others better, leading to more effective communication and relationship management.

Most people who complete the DISC assessment will find that they have one primary style, accompanied by a secondary style. For instance, D as a primary style with S as a secondary style. Such a person will have a set of behavioural traits that are mainly of the D-style and yet tempered by those of an S-style. Typically, such a person may be decisive and results-oriented, yet able to take into account the needs and feelings of his co-workers.

When team leaders and members are aware of the different styles in the team, they frequently marvel at the diversity and richness that is present. Styles are no longer seen in isolation but as a complement to others' styles. For instance, an I- style will now realize that by partnering with a C-style, decisions are made in a more balanced manner. Not purely based on relations and intuition but also on facts and data. A team leader who is a D-style will value the calming and stabilizing presence of an S-style when work is proceeding feverishly.

Frequent points of contention during team sessions can be handled more constructively now as people understand what they may derive from different perspectives. This can lead to more balanced problem-solving and decision-making.

Finally, if we understand style differences, we'll be able to more effectively reconcile opposing views and to influence the other parties. This is done through adapting our approach to address the preferences and needs of others. For instance, if we seek the support and buy-in of a C-style team member, we know that we'll need to be armed with facts and figures to justify our proposal.

ROLES THAT PEOPLE PLAY IN A TEAM

In a team environment, there are certain roles that people prefer to play. What underlines these preferences is a combination of many factors such as experience, aptitude, personality, values, education, etc.

Dr. Meredith Belbin[2] of the United Kingdom has identified nine clusters of behaviours that he calls team roles. He defines team role as "a tendency to behave, contribute and interrelate with others in a particular way."

Belbin classifies the nine clusters into three categories as follows:

- **Action-orientation:** Implementer, Completer-Finisher, Shaper.
- **People-orientation:** Resource-Investigator, Coordinator, Teamworker.
- **Thinking-orientation:** Monitor-Evaluator, Plant, Specialist.

As in behavioural styles, there aren't good or bad team roles. All are useful and different. People have a natural propensity to gravitate towards certain team roles. Each person will not have just one team role but a combination of them. By understanding these team roles, members will be better able to leverage and harness diversity and become a more holistic team.

- Team dynamics are a double-edged sword. They can be a source of competitive advantage or drive team members apart.

- Train your team members to appreciate and manage different individual behavioural styles. Help them understand the different roles that people play in a team.

Q1: Do you know your preferred behavioural style? What about your team members? How will this knowledge help them become more cohesive?

Q2: What are the various team roles that members play in your team? What gaps are there? What can you do about it?

PART FIVE
Managing Key Relationships

2. Managing Team Members

3. Managing Teams

1. Managing Yourself

4. Managing Key Relationships

5. Becoming A More Complete Leader

"You must be the change you want to see in the world."
—Mahatma Gandhi

17 THE POWER OF ENGAGEMENT

THEN AND NOW

I first joined the workforce in the late 1970s. Singapore then was gripped by poverty and the country's unemployment level was high. When I landed my first job as an engineer, I considered myself one of the fortunate few.

It didn't matter that the work environment was noisy and dusty. Or that my boss was insensitive and unapproachable. Life was tough in those days. As job seekers we were looking primarily for three simple things: a source of stable income, a job that was reasonably meaningful and challenging, and a safe working environment.

Thirty years have gone by in a flash. The world has moved on and become a much better place. In today's workforce, there are three broad categories of workers: the Boomers (born between 1946 and 1964), Gen X (born between 1965 and 1980) and Gen Y (born after 1980).

What motivate each of these generational cohorts are very different and yet alike in many ways. The three simple things that satisfied me in my first job will no longer be sufficient for today's workers.

This chapter will discuss the power of engagement. Why is this so important? Because it is the key to unleashing the hidden power in your people. Let's start with a managerial anecdote.

Managerial Anecdote

I first met Sue when she was a newly promoted manager. She was one of the participants attending a transition to management programme that I was conducting for her company's first-time managers. In preparation for the programme, I was briefed by the Learning and Development Manager about the challenges faced by each participant, all of whom were rated as up-and-coming by the company.

Sue was described as "technically brilliant but insensitive to people". In addition, I was told that in the three months since she became a manager, three out of five people in her department had left.

Three years went by since the programme. Recently, I had the opportunity to meet up with Sue again. It was on one of my frequent visits to her company to consult on leadership development. She had just moved another notch up the hierarchy and was now the director of finance and administration. In this capacity she oversaw the work of a group of managers.

The Sue whom I had lunch with that day was a far cry from the person who attended my transition programme a few years before. Prior to our lunch, I had run into a few of her co-workers. All had praises for her ability to bring out the best in her people. In a recent climate survey, the finance division had the best overall results in the company in terms of people engagement.

My interest was naturally piqued. I was all ears as she shared her transformation over the years from "a manager whose only interest was results" to a "manager who strives to inspire and engage her people to achieve their potential".

I asked her what she was doing differently as a manager now compared to then. She quickly reminded me of the concept of "hot buttons" that I had explained to the class. With a smile, she mimicked me, "People are motivated differently. What motivates one person may not motivate another person. As managers we need to find out what our people's hot buttons—their inner-most needs that drive them to do things—are. If we understand these drivers, we can motivate them to go the extra mile."

And that was what she had been doing all this while: working with people to know them, and then creating conditions that help them grow and feel a sense of meaning and achievement in their work.

WHAT IS ENGAGEMENT?

Engagement is the willingness of employees to go beyond the call of duty in their job by contributing more of their energy, creativity and passion. This means exercising discretionary effort for their company.

Why discretionary? Simply because when you deal with knowledge workers, they can either do the bare minimum to meet the requirements of the job, or do much more than that. As the boss, you may notice that George is more productive and creative than John. But you may not know that John is capable of much more than what you have seen because it is all tucked away in his mind.

For many years, many professional services firms such as Towers Perrin (now called Towers Watson), the Gallup Organization and Corporate Executive Board have conducted global workforce studies to understand to what extent employers are achieving the performance that full engagement delivers.

Over the years, the trends shown in these studies have not changed much. The results are quite alarming. Although the statistics will vary from country to country and from Asia, the United States and Europe, the global breakdown from the Towers Perrin 2007–2008 Global Workforce Study[1] shows the following:

- Only one in five workers is willing to go the extra mile for their companies;
- Two out of five workers are capable but not fully committed; and
- Two out of five workers have checked out to some extent, i.e. doing the bare minimum to get by.

In the same study, the findings show:
- Employees care a lot about their work;
- They want to learn and grow;
- They want stability and security;
- With the right opportunities and resources, they'll commit to a career with a company; and
- They care deeply about work-life balance, but they are not, for the most part, slacking off.

IMPORTANCE OF EMPLOYEE ENGAGEMENT

Companies with high employee engagement have an enviable competitive edge. Their organizational performance improves significantly in three key areas: financial results (revenue and profitability), operational results (customer service, quality, innovation and even lower cost) and employee turnover (engaged employees will stay and influence co-workers to do similarly).

WHAT DRIVES EMPLOYEE ENGAGEMENT?

There are three broad drivers of employee engagement as follows:

1. Organizational leadership

This includes the image that senior management projects internally as well as externally. Is the company held in high regard by the local and international community? Do employees respect the senior leaders for the way they act and behave individually as well as in a team? Do the leaders genuinely care about the well-being of the employees? Do they exemplify the corporate values that they espouse?

2. Work environment

Is there an alignment between work activities and business priorities? Do people and departments work well with each other? How committed and competent are your fellow workers? Does the culture encourage open-sharing and innovation? How do you feel at the end of each day? Do you look forward to coming to work every day? How competitive is the pay structure? Is there work-life balance?

3. Care for employees as individuals

How meaningful and challenging is your work? Are you doing things that you are good at? Do you have the facilities that you need to do your work? Are you improving yourself year over year? What are your career advancement opportunities? How's your relationship with your boss? Do your opinions count? Do you feel included?

Looking at the three clusters of drivers, one realizes that senior leadership plays a primary role in creating the conditions that drive engagement. It is both in the interest, as well as the obligation, of senior managers to take these findings on-board and raise the engagement profile of their companies.

Individual managers too have a role to play. Employees for the most part want to be engaged. As seen in the managerial anecdote, you can go a long way towards motivating your people and making it meaningful for them as Sue has done in her own way.

HOW CAN YOU MOTIVATE YOUR PEOPLE?

I recommend a five-step approach:

1. Know them/Know you

Treat your people as individuals. Spend quality time with each person to get to know them and to let them know you. Do this in an authentic and sincere way. In Asia, this is especially important. Subordinates are wary about being seen to cosy up to the boss. Thus, they will keep a discreet distance. As the boss, be the one to initiate one-on-one conversations with your people. Take them out for lunch once a while.

2. Know their hot buttons

Remember that people are motivated differently. If you are motivated by larger responsibilities and more power, it does not mean that the same applies for others. Motivators may be as varied as wishing to work with congenial team mates, opportunities to learn new skills, possibilities for exposure to senior management, promotion, pay raises, overseas travel, better work-life balance, etc.

3. Shape their work appropriately

While it is unrealistic to customize the work for everybody, managers have more latitude than they recognize. If you know the preferred behavioural styles of an individual, you may assign more of certain tasks and less of something else. For instance, in a team environment, you may, with a little more thought and planning, ask a C-style ("Compliant" type as derived from the DISC profile) to take on greater responsibilities for data gathering and analysis while an I-style ("Influencing" type as based on the DISC profile) may be tasked with interfacing with stakeholders outside the team.

4. Coach and develop them

Many managers have one-on-one sessions with their direct reports. But it focuses only on work. I do suggest that you have separate sessions to discuss with each of your people regarding his development. This can take place once a quarter and last no more than 45 minutes. Discuss his aspirations and career goals. Help him identify how he needs to develop himself in order to attain his goals. Connect with your boss and the HR organization as well. Coach your people and facilitate their growth. If they are convinced that you are invested in their development, you will go a long way towards engaging them.

5. Reward and recognition

When your people have done well, pause and express your appreciation to them. Do it in a sincere manner. It matters a lot to people to have their boss acknowledge a job well done. Asians cringe when bosses praise them. They always say, "It's my job," as though they don't expect nor deserve the compliment. Don't take their word for it. It is just modesty which is a cultural trait. Asians especially the Gen-Y love to be praised. For those who are praised, may I suggest that a far better way of responding to a compliment is to say, "Thank you." Bosses, please remember that at the end of the year, when the annual performance review is done, the compensation must be fair and commensurate with the accomplishments. This goes a long way in helping you retain your talent pool.

INTER-GENERATIONAL DIFFERENCES

In today's workplace, the Gen X is sandwiched by the Boomers and

Gen Y. All three cohorts are currently present in sizeable numbers in the workforce. In the years ahead, the Boomers will retire while more Gen-Y will join the workforce. They will increasingly be supplying management and leadership talents. Hence, understanding what generally attracts, engages and retains Gen-Y will be critical to achieving organizational success.

Unlike the Boomers and Gen-X, the Gen-Y have only experienced a life of relative prosperity, socio-economic freedom and financial security. Their perspectives on life and how they view the nuances of the world may therefore be different. They are, generally, also more tech savvy and have different expectations compared to the other generations. Basically, they want success quickly and on their own terms. These will mean career advancement opportunities, competitive pay structure, opportunities to learn and develop themselves, and work-life balance.

Knowing and acting on what drives the Boomers and the Gen-X will be just as important as well. In the multi-generational workforce, there is much that each generation can learn from the other. Leveraging on this diversity will enable organizations to sharpen their competitive edge.

The following table shows the top five engagement factors for a sample distribution across generations. It is adapted from the Towers Perrin report cited earlier.

Table 17.1: Top engagement factors across generations

	GEN Y	GEN X	BOOMERS
1	Have excellent career advancement opportunities	Senior management's interest in employees' well-being	Senior management's interest in employees' well-being
2	Senior management acts to ensure organization's long-term success	Improved my skills and capabilities over last year	Improved my skills and capabilities over last year
3	Organization's reputation for social responsibility	Organization's reputation for social responsibility	Organization's reputation for social responsibility
4	Input into decision-making in my department	Input into decision-making in my department	Input into decision-making in my department
5	Set high professional standards	Organization quickly resolves customer concerns	Challenging work that broadens skills

- The Towers Perrin 2007–08 Workforce Study shows both a bleak picture, as well as a promise, of today's workforce. Only one out of five workers is engaged. Two out of five are willing and waiting to be engaged. And two out of five workers have become disengaged.

- Instead of having only one out of five workers engaged, companies can raise the number to three out of five. By working in concert, top management and line managers can make this happen.

Q1: How engaged are you personally? What drives your engagement?

Q2: Do you know the hot buttons of your people? What will you do to motivate them?

18 LEVERAGING CULTURAL DIVERSITY

A CULTURAL MELTING POT

As globalization gathers pace, it is becoming a norm to see people of different nationalities working side by side at workplaces in most cities around the world. In the virtual work settings, this is even more prevalent. Colleagues whose home locations are many time zones apart and who have never met each other are communicating through teleconferences or web meetings.

In the 21st century, diversity will become a defining feature of worklife. As managers, what should our attitude be towards diversity? Will work be more productive and satisfying if our co-workers think and act alike? Or is it better to have a diverse team? Before we consider these questions, let us understand why we think and behave differently.

THE WAY WE SEE THE WORLD

The way individuals view the world depend on a number of factors. Please refer to the diagram below.

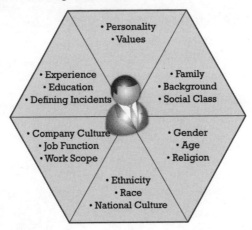

• Personality
• Values

• Experience
• Education
• Defining Incidents

• Family
• Background
• Social Class

• Company Culture
• Job Function
• Work Scope

• Gender
• Age
• Religion

• Ethnicity
• Race
• National Culture

Diagram 18.1: Personal Filter

The confluence of all these factors will shape the way we view the world. They create a kind of personal filter which we all carry around with us unconsciously. Each time, we experience or witness an event, we interpret it through this filter. And it's important to realize that it is essentially only one way of interpretation—our own. To us, it is the truth. Others who look at that same event will have a different view though. And to them, that's their truth.

Without realizing it, we may become stuck with our own view. It is important to remind ourselves that our view is neither the only nor always the best view. The more ways we can look at a situation, the more possibilities we'll discover and the more creative we can be.

Let's look at what transpired at a management meeting of a healthcare company when temper ran a little high and some key players were jostling with each other to influence the boss to adopt their recommendations.

Managerial Anecdote

It was the weekly senior management meeting of the city's largest and most successful chain of personal healthcare stores. The people in attendance made for a truly multicultural assembly. The GM, Yoko san, herself was Japanese. Her directors were Chinese, English, Indian, American and Thai.

One of the key items on the agenda was "Measures to raise productivity". Three directors had presented their proposals and a lively discussion ensued. Yoko san listened carefully to the various views and encouraged everybody to participate actively. She asked many thoughtful questions and did not seem ready to accept any particular recommendation.

As the meeting drew to a close, she thanked the people present and requested all members to consider the various options carefully over the weekend and be prepared to make a decision the following week.

As people streamed out of the conference room, two directors were exchanging notes with each other. The Operations Director, Chan, a Hong Kong-born Chinese who was responsible for the day-to-day management of the hundred-odd outlets, said that the GM was indecisive and should have endorsed his proposal without any more delay. Time after all was of the essence.

Sandra, the English HR director, thought differently. She felt that their boss was right to hear everyone out and to encourage some reflection over the weekend before making the final decision. The changes contemplated would have a major impact on the future of the chain and the morale of the workforce.

It was the same meeting and yet a sampling of two participants' reaction revealed different perspectives on what had transpired. How does one account for these differing viewpoints?

We all interpret things in our own unique way. Though there will be nuances in the way we see things, in most situations and to varying degree, people are willing to give and take a little. But when we have a vested interest in what is happening, we become more touchy and assertive.

Chan, the Operations Director who was under pressure to raise productivity, obviously was more antsy and wanted to move faster. Sandra, the HR director, on the other hand, was not on the firing line and could sit back and take a broader view. Ensuring that the people side of business was accorded due consideration was her job. Hence, she favoured more deliberation.

A couple of questions come to one's mind while considering the difference of opinions between the two directors. Firstly, did their different ethnicity have any bearing on their viewpoints? Secondly, was their company better served because of their diverse views?

Clearly, the answer to the first question is that ethnicity had at most an indirect influence on their different viewpoints. The key driver was their job functions. There is a saying worth bearing in mind, "Where we stand depends on where we sit."

As to the second question, it is undeniable that it is always better to have different perspectives when it comes to important matters such as the topic being tabled. When differing ideas are expressed, the discussions become more interesting and animated. It is in such an atmosphere of spirited inquiry that creative solutions may emerge.

Let's now consider a situation where cultural differences may influence our perspectives significantly.

EAST VS WEST

In many traffic-congested cities in Asia,[1] car drivers, pedestrians and cyclists are up in arms against each other. An alarming number of cyclists and pedestrians lose their lives each year to thoughtless drivers who feel that roads belong to cars—especially their cars.

Authorities are under pressure to build proper cycling lanes, install more pedestrian crossings, underpasses, overhead bridges and implement clearer rules on how all road users can coexist. In other words, in Asian societies which tend to be more conformist, the conventional thinking is that more rules and clearer lane demarcation will make for safer roads for all road users. While the public discourse continues, pedestrians and cyclists continued to feel aggrieved in cities such Bangkok, Taipei, Singapore, Kuala Lumpur, Mumbai, Shanghai, etc.

In the other half of the hemisphere, in some towns in Holland, France and Germany, a diametrically opposite approach is favoured by some people. Traffic authorities have removed traffic lights, road markings and some pedestrian crossings. It is no longer clear who has the right of way nor how fast drivers can go.

One would have thought that anarchy would have reigned supreme. Yet the opposite effect is seen. Traffic becomes smoother because drivers consciously slow down. Cyclists and pedestrians are also more cautious and alert. All parties now make eye contact with each other as they negotiate the ambiguous space in front of them. In other words, the town is now safer for all road users because nobody has the right of way.

CULTURAL DIVERSITY AS A
SOURCE OF COMPETITIVE ADVANTAGE

The traffic example shows how cultural differences may shape our thinking. To be sure, national culture and ethnicity are only two of the many components that make up our personal world view. Nonetheless, they do provide richness, nuances and colours in the tapestry of ideas that leaders and their teams need to weave.

Yoko san, the GM featured in the managerial anecdote explained to me that her job is rewarding and satisfying because she has a diverse team of outstanding people. Not only are they all very competent in their respective field, they also bring their uniqueness to the company—their life experiences, personalities and their national cultures. Thus, they all tend to think and behave differently towards work and people. And that's the reason she always encourages different perspectives and will hear everyone out.

Different ways of knowing make us wiser.

She said, "There have been many occasions when we were hopelessly deadlocked, and then someone expressed an opinion that was a new insight for us all. This is what I wish to see more of during our meetings. When we explore different perspectives, our solutions are richer."

Neither the Western nor the Eastern way of attending to reality is right or wrong, good or bad, per se. Some years ago, Professor Kaiping Peng from China said to Professor Richard Nisbett of the United States, "You know, the difference between you and me is that I think the world is a circle, and you think it's a line."[2]

As long as they are good ideas, does it matter whether it's a circle or a line? Whether considered in a linear or holistic approach, ideas are the new currency. That's why communities around the world which open their doors to talent, regardless of nationalities, are thriving. Contrast California with Japan.

I would like to wrap this chapter up with a quote that aptly summarizes our discussions.

"The mind, once expanded to the dimensions of larger ideas,
never returns to its original size."
— Oliver Wendell Holmes

- Our view is determined by our personal filter. It's just one view and may not be the only or best view.

- Cultural diversity provides richness, nuances and colours in the tapestry of ideas that individuals and teams need to weave.

Q1: How culturally diverse is your team now? What can you do to encourage greater diversity?

Q2: To experience the power of ideas, log onto http://www.ted.com

19 MANAGING CONFLICT

WHY CONFLICT ARISES

In work as well as in life, conflict is inevitable. Much as we try to avoid it, there will be many situations when people have opposing needs, differing viewpoints, different priorities, or incompatible goals, interests, principles or feelings. When such people meet, conflict frequently erupts.

As managers, we have to learn to deal with conflict. Team members, in the course of their interaction, will run into conflict with each other. You will also encounter situations where you don't see eye to eye with your subordinates, peers, bosses and other stakeholders. Ditto for relationships with customers and vendors. Being able to manage conflict will be instrumental in making your team more effective. It is also a prerequisite for effectively influencing others and winning their support.

HOW DO PEOPLE RESPOND TO CONFLICT?

Most of us dread conflict. Our experience with it is unlikely to be pleasant. But must conflict always lead to tensions, anger and hard-feelings? Is there any possibility that some good may arise from conflict? It really depends on how we handle it.

While conflict is inevitable, the outcome need not be destructive. It is possible to prevent this emotionally wrenching yet inescapable facet of human interaction from holding us hostage, bedevilling relationships and causing long-term damage.

Let's start by understanding how people typically react when faced with a conflict. Most of us instinctively think that the two most common modes are fight or flight. According to Thomas and Kilmann, there are five conflict handling modes as shown in the following diagram:

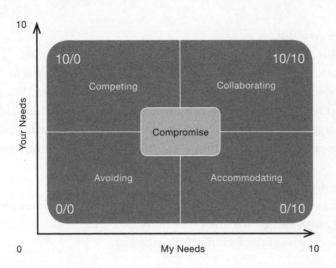

Diagram 19.1: The Five Conflict-Handling Modes

10/0—Competing

This is the fight response. This person will use whatever means at his disposal to win at the expense of the other party. When this mode is invoked, relationship and trust become eroded. The discussions quickly spiral out of control. It is unlikely that people will remain open and receptive when emotions are running high. The topic on hand will thus not get a balanced hearing. More likely than not, it will result in a deadlock. If the person who adopts this take-no-prisoner tactic appears to have gained the upper hand, his victory will be short-lived. The bad feelings generated may prevent people from working effectively with each other henceforth. People have long memories. Their day will come.

0/10—Accommodating

This is the opposite of competing. In this stance, this person basically sacrifices his needs in order to appease the other party. When a person adopts this mode, he is essentially short-changing himself and his own needs. His self-esteem will be impacted and others may lose respect for him as well.

0/0—Avoiding

This is the flight response. Basically, this person opts out of the argument and chooses to remain silent. Or it could take the form of sidestepping the issues or postponing it for another time. Managers who choose to take this stance are electing not to share their side of the argument. It may be to buy time to gather their thoughts before responding, or simply withdrawing from a threatening situation.

5/5—Compromsing

This is seeking the middle-ground, by making trade-offs. Some people may adopt this stance when they think that splitting the differences is the only way out of a difficult situation.

10/10—Collaborating

This is going for the win-win, working with the other party to find a solution that satisfies the needs of both parties. In this mode, conflict is viewed positively as a natural part of human relationship. It is an opportunity to reconcile opposing needs and can indeed be a springboard for deepening the relationships between colleagues. By engaging each other with mutual respect, empathy and openness, they hope to reach a win-win situation.

> *"Without a fight, people will not know each other."*
> — Old Chinese saying

Let's now take a look at a typical workplace conflict in the following managerial anecdote.

Managerial Anecdote

Shin, a new sales manager, could hardly hide his excitement when he secured a trial order from a client whom he was courting for a few months. It could potentially turn into a major account for the company. His excitement however quickly turned into dismay when he went to speak to the production controller Jodie who was responsible for scheduling fulfilment of customer orders through the factory.

Jodie basically said that the factory was already running at full capacity for the next three months. The earliest that she could schedule the run for Shin would be 10 weeks from now.

Shin became upset and raised his voice. He accused Jodie of being unresponsive to customer needs. He had already promised his customer that he could arrange for his order to be shipped within a month. Jodie, who was a veteran in the company, dug in her heels and refused to budge. She retorted that before accepting any new orders, sales people should have checked with her department.

The shouting match led nowhere. Shin soon left in a huff to escalate the matter to his boss.

A CONFLICT-RESOLUTION FRAMEWORK[1]

Let's now consider how conflicts may be resolved more productively by using a conflict-resolution framework. The four recommended steps are as follows:

Step 1: Stay composed

When we are in a conflict, the natural tendency is to feel threatened and behave as though we are under siege. Our body tenses, our mouth becomes dry and adrenalin is pumping. Our brain becomes hijacked by emotions. This will lead to what is called the fight or flight response. Or we may default into one of the three other modes as discussed earlier.

We need to heed the unmistakable signs that our body is sending us. Be aware that we are under stress. Then tell ourselves that we will remain calm and collected. This is self-regulation.

When Shin was told by Jodie that the factory could not ship his new order within a month, he was obviously upset. This is a critical moment. If he lost control of his emotions, as he did, the conflict would escalate. The more effective approach was to pause and stay composed.

Step 2: Seek to understand

While remaining calm, let's put ourselves in the shoes of the other person and seek to understand where she is coming from. Consciously separate the person from the issue. This is a good way to avoid personalizing the conflict.

Do not assume that the other person is just being intransigent or trying to sabotage what you are doing. She may be driven by other concerns and constraints that you may not be aware of. In other words, do we understand her perspective?

For example, Shin might have asked himself, "Why is Jodie unable to fit my client's order into the production pipeline in the next thirty days? Does she not realize that this may potentially be a major account? How may I work with her to get this order fulfilled in time without upsetting her overall production schedule?"

By adopting this line of genuine inquiry, Shin would have reframed the situation from one in which Jodie was simply uncooperative for reasons that only she knew to one in which he was seeking to understand the drivers behind Jodie's response.

For instance, Shin might have said, "I realize now that there are difficulties scheduling my client's order into the system in the next thirty days. As I'm still new to the company, can you please explain the constraints to me?"

Jodie might then say that the company's production schedule was done on a four-week rolling forecast basis. As customers demands had been rising, capacity was now booked for the next three months. Hence she could not schedule a run for Shin's order in the next 30 days.

Step 3: Explore options

Having paused to reflect and reframe, we are now better prepared mentally and emotionally to engage the other party more constructively. Some key competencies that we may draw upon are the coaching proficiencies that we have already discussed quite extensively. Specifically they are trust- and rapport-building, listening, questioning and the judicious use of silence

By seeking to understand the other party, we are building an emotional connection with her. When the other party discerns that you are sincere and open, she will become less on the edge and will start to become more conciliatory and measured in her tone, words and gestures.

Similarly when you genuinely understand the other person's perspective, you'll sense that her concerns are valid. Suddenly it may dawn upon Shin he had been remiss in not checking with her before accepting the order. To apologize for this oversight would be a reasonable thing to do.

He could then explain to her the situation with his client and that this trial order could potentially turn into a key account. No one could really tell how Jodie would respond. However, if the conversation so far had been managed constructively, this additional bit of information on the potential of this account might elicit greater willingness by Jodie to help him out.

Invite the other party to participate in moving the problem to solution. Share your own suggestions as well.

Step 4: Agree and commit

The final step is to evaluate the various options and to agree what the next step is. The ideal outcome is to have a win-win for both parties. Sometimes, you may end up getting slightly less than what you had hoped for. For instance, the best that Jodie could do was to schedule his customer's order within six weeks. Though this was not exactly meeting Shin's commitment to his customer, it was much better than the original 10 weeks.

When resolving conflicts, one has to view the incident on a broader canvass and with a longer horizon. In the months and years ahead, there will be other occasions for both Shin and Jodie to engage each other. When the discussion wraps up, make sure that sufficient goodwill has been built up. You may need to draw upon it the next time. This is the concept of building an emotional bank account.

PRE-EMPTING CONFLICTS

When disagreement occurs between people who know each other and have some mutual trust, it is far easier to come to a common ground than between people who do not know each other. Hence don't wait for crises to erupt before attending to a relationship.

Proactively identify your key interfaces and know where tension and disagreement may potentially erupt. These are organizational fault lines, if you will. It is not uncommon for managers in different departments to collide with each other on account of their key performance indicators or KPIs. For instance, a common manufacturing KPI is to reduce the unit cost of production. Hence, they prefer long production runs with less product variety. On the other hand, a common marketing KPI is customer satisfaction. Thus they would like to have a wide variety of products available. Between manufacturing and marketing lies an organization fault line. Another such fault line is the intersection between sales and production control in our anecdote.

It therefore behooves managers who are located along such organizational fault lines to invest in building relationship with each other. Spend time knowing each other as individuals and appreciate each other's KPIs and pressure points. Through frequent interaction and experiencing the way each other behaves, a sense of common purpose and rapport will gradually manifest. Recognize that in order to succeed, you need to work in collaboration with others. It is not a zero sum game.

- Conflicts are inevitable in work and life. We can however, learn to manage it so that the outcome is productive for all parties concerned.

- The four-step conflict-resolution framework will help you work towards a win-win solution for all parties.

Q1: When you are in a conflict, what modes do you habitually adopt? How useful has it been for you?

Q2: The next time you get into a conflict, practise using the conflict-resolution framework. Evaluate the results and compare them with what you had experienced in Q1.

CHANGE IS THE ONLY CONSTANT

The only constant these days is change, as the saying goes. And for managers the ability to lead change is becoming a core competency. To be sure, we aren't advocating change for change's sake. Rather, we are simply recognizing that it is the only way to stay ahead.

For instance, when you assume responsibility for leading your team of five persons, you may realize within a short while that there are some glaring inefficiencies in the way responsibilities are distributed among your subordinates. As a result, some people are overworked while others seem to be having an easy time. This is the legacy you have inherited from the previous manager who has moved on. Now what?

You can either maintain the status quo or make changes to put things right. What will you do? Either approach will have its consequences. Deciding to do nothing will impact the team's overall productivity. Ultimately, the buck will stop at your door. That's why you're the boss. And if you decide to make changes, it isn't going to be easy as well.

Consider this quote written 500 years ago:

"There is nothing more difficult to carry out, nor more doubtful of success, nor more dangerous to handle than to initiate a new order of things. For the reformer has enemies in all those who could benefit by the old order, and only lukewarm defenders by all those who could benefit by the new order. This lukewarmness arises from the incredulity of mankind who do not truly believe in anything new until they have had actual experience with it."

— Niccolo Machiavelli

HOW DO PEOPLE REACT TO CHANGE?

Clearly, resistance to change is not a 21st century phenomenon. It has been biologically hard-wired in humans through the ages. That's how mankind has survived: by hanging on to what has worked in the past as it gives us a sense of comfort and security. Most of us aren't too keen to try new ways because none of us really knows whether they will work. Better to be safe than sorry, many would think.

Just look back at your leadership journey since you became a manager. Much as you have realized that as you move higher up, you will have to behave differently, how easy has it been for you to let go of old ways of doing things?

When people are faced with change, they will react in a predictable manner as they go through a state of transition (Bridges and Mitchell). There are three phases as Diagram 20.1 illustrates.

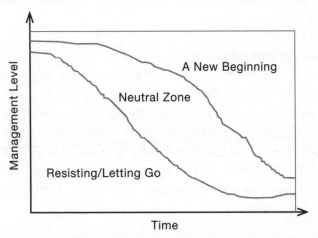

Diagram 20.1: The change model

Phase 1: Letting go
When people are faced with change, the instinctive response is to deny that change is necessary. Letting go is difficult because you are asking them to abandon the old and familiar for the unknown

and uncertain. It means not doing things that have made them successful. Relationship, routine and work environment may no longer be the same. Hence their whole world of experience, their identity and indeed their reality, will be impacted.

Phase 2: Shifting into neutral zone
Even as people reluctantly agree to let go of old ways, it does not mean they know what the new ways are or how to embrace them. The neutral zone is fraught with uncertainty and doubts. There is a lot of struggle going on. In fact, people may move two steps forward and take one step backwards. This also represents a time and opportunity for people to face up to their inner fears and discover new energy and purpose. Sufficient time should be allowed for people to come to terms with the need to change and deal with themselves. Leaders need to be patient. If done well, people will be better prepared for the third phase.

Phase 3: Moving forward
When the leader and his people have hashed out all the concerns that have surfaced, they will enter the third phase where they are ready for a new beginning. This is where people shift from reflection and contemplation to the more practical aspects of implementation and making the change work. It is tough because in trying out new ways, mistakes will be made and progress may be slow. Leaders need to demonstrate a sense of optimism while providing support.

HOW CAN MANAGERS LEAD CHANGE MORE EFFECTIVELY?
Many well-intentioned managers literally gush with excitement about ideas that they would like to implement. Resistance as we have said is to be expected. However, if they recognize the following principles governing change, their chances for garnering support and buy-in will be much greater:

- Slow down and let people catch up. The higher up the management level you are, the more ready you are to bring about change. That's because you already have had a lot of time to reconcile mentally and emotionally with the idea of change. When you talk to your people, realize that you are ahead of the curve. Therefore, don't rush. Allow sufficient time for your people to catch up.
- Know that it's natural for people to resist change. Anticipate this and be prepared to address their concerns.
- When change is contemplated, two forces are at work in opposition to each other. Restraining forces comprise fears, doubts, uncertainties, insecurities, etc. The driving forces will be all the good that the change will bring. Persuasion is possible only if your constituents believe that the benefits outweigh the costs involved, especially personal costs. Personal costs may the following: (a) giving up the familiar and comfortable, (b) overseeing fewer people, which means a loss of status and face, (c) needing to learn new skills while fearful that one may not be able to make it, etc.
- Your team will not change unless the individual members change. Only by changing them, or the way they think and behave, can you change the team or the organization.

The following describes a framework for effectively leading and managing change.

THE CHANGE MANAGEMENT FRAMEWORK[1]

1. Explain why the change is necessary

Do it in a compelling and succinct manner. Take no more than a few minutes. State clearly: What is the change? Why is it needed? What will be the consequences if we don't change? What are the benefits if we change?

2. Provide sufficient information about the change

Share information about what the change entails: what, who, when, where and how. Discuss the rationale. Openly explain your own perspectives. Address the pros and cons for making the change. Tell your people why you are in favour of going ahead.

3. Allow time to surface and address concerns

Encourage people to ask questions about how the change will affect them personally. Not everybody is comfortable speaking up though. Hopefully before the meeting on change takes place, you would have established a sense of trust and rapport with your team members.

At this point, your ability to listen, be empathetic, ask questions and provide space for people to voice their innermost thoughts will be vital. Watch and observe how people are reacting. Not everybody responds the same way. Some are more ready to express their thoughts than others.

These are some common questions. Not all will be articulated though. You may even have to tease them out of the people.

- How will I be equipped with the new skills required?
- In the new set-up, I think my scope of work is reduced. I will lose face.
- You are asking me to do more than in the past. What's in it for me (WIIFM)?
- I'm really uncomfortable. I'm not sure that I can do it.
- Will there be additional resources that I can draw on?

It is sensible to adjourn the discussions at the end of Step 3. Let them mull over what you have said for a few days before resuming discussions and moving on to Step 4. It is unlikely that you have heard and addressed everything. Use the breaks in discussions to speak to the more quiet ones individually. Also, you may know that some team members have greater influence over others. Seek these informal leaders out and ask them for their opinions. Incorporate suggestions from them. Co-opt them as allies.

Encourage people to talk among themselves. Tell them you are also available for informal chats. Once you sense that people are letting go of the past, start involving them in planning the implementation.

4. Communicate the implementation plan

At the resumption of discussions, invite thoughts and questions. Perhaps, this is where you may request the influential informal leaders to share their views. A word from one of the guys, especially a well-respected one, may sometimes carry more weight than the same from someone who represents management: you.

The leader will now outline the overall implementation plan, calling out the key areas. Involve other members to explain the execution. Invite input and tweak where necessary. Maximize participation so that everyone has a role to play. Create a sense of ownership by letting people be responsible for different parts of the plan.

Listen and ask questions. Then end with an action plan with milestones and accountabilities defined.

5. Generate and celebrate small wins

Have regular progress reviews with your people. Expect some teething issues. Help the team address these. Also, some people may not be progressing as fast as others. Be patient and provide support. It is better to speak individually to team members who need more attention from you. Remember to carry out your part of the bargain to provide training and other support, and gather the team to celebrate small wins. This will be a booster that individuals and the team as a whole need.

6. Debrief and refine

When the change has been completely implemented, invite the team to share lessons learnt. Recognize the team for their contribution. Discuss how the plan can be further refined to be even more effective. Encourage shared leadership, i.e. all members have to feel that they have ownership in the overall success and that they can make a difference by offering suggestions. Again, remember to celebrate success.

There will be times when some team members just simply refuse to go along with the change that is necessary. What then do you do? This is another instance when you may need to have a difficult conversation.

- Although it is necessary to keep changing in order to stay ahead, people will naturally resist change.

- All changes start with the individuals. If they don't change, the teams or organizations will not change. The change management framework will help you to lead and manage change effectively.

Q1: When was the last time a change was implemented in your company? How well was the change communicated and implemented?

Q2: If you were tasked with leading the change in Q1, how would you approach it?

21 HOW TO INFLUENCE

BUT FIRST, HOW NOT TO INFLUENCE

Let's start with an anecdote on how one manager tried to influence her team into agreeing and working towards a new vision.

Managerial Anecdote

Shirley was one of the brightest stars in the company. At the age of 31, she was appointed the GM of the largest division, replacing the incumbent who was her boss. The division was underperforming in his short-lived 18-month tenure.

True to her reputation as a go-getter, she was chomping at the bit as she stepped into her new role. At the end of the first week, she gathered her team and announced her vision for the division.

It was an ambitious plan that would require 150 percent effort from everybody. The division would grow much faster, and out-perform all other similar divisions in the group in Southeast Asia within two years. She planned to restructure and recruit new people.

Shirley had painted a bold vision for the division. She really wanted to revitalize her people and inject a sense of purpose and hope. The team members listened attentively but said little otherwise. Perhaps, they needed more time to digest this, Shirley reasoned to herself.

That evening, she invited Jin Lin for a chat. Jin Lin had been her peer for three years before Shirley got promoted. While Shirley was exuberant and wanted to know the people's reaction, Jin Lin was strangely quiet. It was only after much coaxing that she let on, "I don't think the team members are on-board with you. You are moving too fast."

In the work that I do with managers, I have had the unfortunate experience of witnessing how people flounder when they need to influence. The anecdote illustrates a typical example of a ham-fisted attempt at influencing.

COMMON MISTAKES THAT MANAGERS MAKE

1. Rely on their position and authority

Managers assume that as they are the boss, they know all the answers and that their people are there to do as they are told. This is the style of the command-and-control managers who get things done through the exercise of hard power. When people comply with the boss's instructions, they do so only because they have to, not because they want to.

Remember: When "No" is not an option,
"Yes" does not mean anything.

2. It is an argument based on facts, figures and logic

Some managers approach discussions with everything figured out, or so it seems. As they speak, they provide facts and figures to back up what they say. Yet, as you listen, you don't really buy their argument. Something is missing. And you know it in your guts.

3. It's a one-shot effort

Influencing is a process, not an event. Rarely is it possible to reach a common understanding at the first try. It involves a lot of listening and seeking others' opinions, then tweaking your original idea and seeking a new position that incorporates their input. Compromising and reworking are part of the influencing process.

4. They come in cold

In this situation, you can sense that these managers are ill-prepared. Though they have a view to present, they have little knowledge of their audience. As they don't know what their interests and concerns are, they lose the opportunity to establish a common ground with their team workers. They may even walk onto a landmine.

EIGHT LEVERS OF INFLUENCE[1]

For the past six decades, behavioural scientists have done studies that shed light on how certain interactions lead people to agree, concede, comply or change. They are able to demonstrate that influence works by appealing to a limited set of deeply rooted human needs and drives in a predictable way. By understanding these basic principles and applying them appropriately, managers can become more effective in influencing others. There are eight levers of influence you can use:

Lever 1: Position

This is hard power. It comes from your position in the organization. The more senior you are in the hierarchy, the greater is the authority that you wield. Intuitively we think that the boss will know more as he is closer to the powers that be and will be privy to confidential information we lack.

Lever 2: Credibility

If you are known to possess expertise and a track record in a particular field, your opinion will travel further and carry more weight. For instance, if you have had many years of working in China to successfully grow a fast-food business from the ground up, your credibility is high when you speak on this topic. In many parts of the world, age has the same effect. In Asia, we also tend to defer to people with grey hair because we expect that they will have more battle scars to show, as well as richer experience and wisdom to tap on.

Lever 3: Network

This comes from your association with respected people. There is much truth in the saying that "It's not just what you know but also who you know." If the person whom you are trying to influence knows you as someone reliable, objective and trustworthy, half the battle is already won. Relationship also comes in the form of your network of friends and powerful people inside and outside the company. Two examples: (a) Young managers who have senior leaders who mentor them and act as their sponsors will find their career paths much smoother. (b) If you, as a manager, have a strong network of other managers in various parts of the company, you can open up doors for your subordinates when they need help. As such, your subordinates will hold you in high regard.

In China, relationship is called *guanxi*. It is an important element in doing business with the Chinese.

> *"At home, you may rely on family members.*
> *Away from home, you need to rely on friends."*
> — Old Chinese saying

Lever 4: Reputation
This is soft power that derives from personal attributes such as character, trustworthiness, approachability, kindness, sense of humour, etc. If you wish to be more influential, make more friends. As human beings, we are partial to people whom we know and like. That's the reason why managers should invest time in getting to know their subordinates, peers and bosses one-on-one. On the flip-side, if you have a tense and unproductive relationship with another manager, don't be surprised if he does not support you when you need him.

> *"Better to have one more friend than one more enemy."*
> — Old Chinese saying

Lever 5: Reciprocity
This is a basic principle in human interaction. It is almost a universal belief in all societies that when we do something for someone, that person will repay us in kind sometime later. It is *quid pro quo*. Take for example, during a recent management meeting, you had difficulty justifying your request to add a temporary headcount to complete an urgent piece of work. A colleague chimed in to

support your request. That clinched it for you. You naturally felt very appreciative of her gesture. When an opportunity presented itself, you returned the favour, didn't you?

In China, reciprocity is called *hui bao*. Favours are always remembered and returned, although not right away. This principle is very important and has application in a variety of relationships in today's organization context. We'll have more to say about this in the following two chapters on managing key stakeholders.

Lever 6: Giving face

In all Asian cultures, there is the notion of "face". It is *mianzi* in China, *omoiyari* in Japan, *pakikisama* in the Philippines, *kibun* in Korea and *krengchai* in Thailand. Face is closely associated with the concept of dignity and prestige. It also defines a person's place or status in a social network. For instance, you are a sales manager and have been working out the details of a service agreement with a customer. Your point of contact is the purchasing manager there. Everything is finalized and all that is left is to ink the deal officially. The date is fixed. The purchasing manager's boss, the General Manager, will be present. If you turn up to sign the agreement on behalf of your company, it may be a *faux pas*. Invite a senior leader instead. Perhaps your Managing Director. Doing so is to give face to the GM.

Lever 7: Peer pressure

Human beings are social creatures. We are heavily influenced by the cues sent by people around us on what we should do and how we should think. Especially if they are our peers. Imagine that you are trying to streamline the processes in your dept. A few people are resisting. You are about to launch into an impassioned appeal for their support. Fortunately for you, a well-respected old-timer who supports the change decides to speak up before you do. This may turn out to be more effective than that speech from you. Sometimes, an indirect strategy works better.

Lever 8: Emotional connection

Because we are basically driven more by our emotions than we are willing to admit, if you wish to influence someone, using cold logic alone will not do it. People not only have to "see" the message, they need to "feel" it. We therefore need to sense their mood and tailor our approach to connect with them emotionally, as discussed in the chapter on EQ. Empathy is crucial for wielding influence. The first step is to read emotional cues and build rapport. In so doing, you would have found out more about the situation and about the people involved, even before attempting to influence. Know their key hot buttons. Empathizing requires time and may even seem to be a detour but it really is an essential step.

Once you have established common grounds, you may then decide on what your influence strategy is. When you win them over, it will be because you have engaged not only their heads but their hearts.

CLOSING WORDS

People who are effective at influencing do not rely on a single lever of influence. They marshal several of them at once to achieve better results.

It is also important to note that there is a big difference between influencing and manipulating. When you influence, it is usually done for the benefit of both the other party and you. When you manipulate, however, you feign interest in the other party in order to have them buy into your idea. The truth will surface sooner than you know, and out goes your credibility.

But how do you influence peers, bosses and people over whom you have no authority? In the next two chapters, we shall discuss this very common dilemma in the matrix structure of today's work environment.

- Many leaders reply mainly on their positions in order to get things done. In the networked economy, doing so will limit one's effectiveness.

- Know and develop proficiency in all eight levers of influence. Marshal as many of them as you think appropriate to achieve better outcomes.

Q1: Why was Shirley unable to win her people to her vision?

Q2: When you encounter a situation when you need to influence, try using the eight levers discussed. Then evaluate how effective you become when using them.

THE BOSS-SUBORDINATE RELATIONSHIP[1]

In this and the subsequent chapters, we'll be focusing on managing relationship with key stakeholders. You will realize by now, your effectiveness as a manager is very much influenced by the people around you. Let's now discuss that all-important person in your work-life—your boss.

Managerial Anecdote

It was 11 a.m., a little too late for a coffee break and too early for lunch. In the far end of the company cafeteria sat two managers deep in discussion with each other. They both worked for John, who had recently been transferred from London to head the operations in Hong Kong. It had been three months. Already, both were missing their previous boss, Jackie, who had taken on a posting to Taipei.

Manager 1: *I really wish Jackie were still our boss. When he was in charge, directions were clear and we knew what he wanted. He generally left us alone to do our work. We only needed to check in with him on important matters.*

Manager 2: *I can't agree more. John has a different personality. He wants to be kept posted on everything that we do. Maybe it's because he's new and is still adjusting. Besides, Hong Kong is new to him. This is his first Asian assignment.*

Manager 1: *But it's been three months already. Although he's from the United Kingdom, he's not new to our company. I think this is just his behavioural style. He drills down very deep on everything. Doesn't he realize that we are*

very competent and experienced? I wonder
how he finds time to micromanage and still
do his job as our director.

Manager 2: I'm actually quite alarmed by the way he
goes directly to my people. Sometimes, he
even summons them to his office to talk.
While I have no problem with him getting
to know my guys, I think he is causing
confusion lower down the chain. Only this
morning, he asked one of my guys to drop what
he was doing and take on a new task. And I
was not kept informed at all until my guys
came to me in a state of agitation.

The lunch crowd was starting to stream in. As they carried away
their trays, the two managers both agreed that they had to reach
out to John and establish a mutual understanding on how to work
together. Perhaps, it would be better to do it one-on-one as they
didn't want their boss to think that they were ganging up on him. But
talk they must before things spun out of control.

It is obvious John and his two managers weren't in sync with
each other. If this disconnection continued, it would not be a
pretty picture. This is not atypical of relationship between bosses
and subordinates, especially when they are new to each other.
Unfortunately, in many instances, the parties involved fail to
recognize that this can't continue for too long. Over many months,
mistrust builds up and soon the relationship becomes dysfunctional.
There will be many casualties. Mostly, it's the subordinates who will
bear the brunt of it. But the bosses will not be unscathed either.

MYTHS ABOUT THE
BOSS-SUBORDINATE RELATIONSHIP

The two managers in our anecdote were clearly mature and clear-headed people. Once they realized that they and their boss weren't on the same page, they decided that it was their responsibility to reach out to their boss. Not all managers are like this though. These are some common myths about the boss-subordinate relationship.

Myth 1: It is the responsibility of my boss to manage me
As a manager, I do a good job in managing my subordinates. Therefore, I assume that my boss should manage me. Far be it for me to manage my boss!

Myth 2: My boss knows what she is doing
Whatever is happening now, there is a good reason. In due course, she will let me know.

Myth 3: What worked with my old boss will work with my new boss
By applying the same working style with my new boss, I should be fine.

Myth 4: No worries! We've agreed on objectives and deliverables.
By meeting all these, she and I will be in alignment.

Myth 5: My boss sees and knows all the goings-on in our organization
I should not flood her with unnecessary details.

HOW TO BUST THE MYTHS AND MANAGE YOUR BOSS
1. The relationship between a boss and her subordinate is one of mutual dependence
Both need each other to succeed. If you, the subordinate, senses that the relationship is bumpy, be proactive. It is you who must begin to manage it! Don't wait for her to approach you. By then, it may be too late. Trust your intuition.

2. Your boss is not a super being who knows all and sees all

Like you, she is fallible. She also has insecurities and blind spots. Like you, she has a boss who may have high expectations of her. She is likely to be under pressure and is struggling to cope. In fact, her challenges will be greater than yours. When strange and contradictory instructions come from her, don't assume that it is all part of a grand master plan. Approach her to seek clarification.

3. What worked with your old boss may not work with your new boss

They are different people with different personalities. Seek to understand your boss. Know her behavioural style. Find out how she'd like information to be presented. Some like written information. Others prefer face-to-face discussions. There are some who prefer a combination of both. Try to figure out what her DISC profile is. Be ready to adapt your style to suit that of your boss.

4. An agreement about KPIs does not equate to alignment

Defining KPIs with your boss is a one-time event. Being in alignment with your boss is an on-going process. In an organization, the situation changes day by day. What was important last month may be of lesser importance today. Your boss's KPIs may therefore be subject to change as well. Stay in touch with her regularly. In addition, observe how she communicates with others during meetings. Pay attention to what her peers and other senior managers say and do. Develop greater political awareness (more on this in Chapter 24). By piecing all these together, you will stay on top of the situation.

5. The level of details that you provide your boss will be situational

Logically speaking, bosses should not be too concerned with unnecessary details. However, how much she needs may depend on the situation that she's in. For instance, she may have to brief her boss who is a micromanager and she wants to be prepared. Or it could be that she's new and wishes to have a deeper understanding of what is happening. Since she thinks you are a big-picture person who delegates a lot to your people, she therefore decides to bypass you and speak directly to your people. Find out when and to what extent she needs details. Agree on a way to provide what she needs. Things may change as both you and your boss get more comfortable with each other.

6. Know her, know you
If you want to have a productive and mutually supportive relationship with your boss, get to know her and win her trust. This is similar to what you have done with your subordinates and other stakeholders. This is not apple-polishing.

Understand the dos and don'ts of the boss-subordinate relationship. Be dependable. Keep her in the loop. No surprises. Don't over-promise and under-deliver. Very importantly agree on how to break bad news to her. Be realistic. Things will never go completely according to plans. Much as some bosses don't like bad news, it is still your job to let her know before her bosses find out.

7. Know her KPIs and pressure points
Help your boss to succeed. In turn, she will help you to succeed. Remember Lever 5 (Reciprocity) from Chapter 21?

8. Learn how to manage conflict productively with your boss
Both of you need to be open with each other and be willing to express differences of opinion. As we have discussed previously, by managing conflict constructively, creative ideas will emerge.

But it's not an easy thing to do. Asians typically do not wish to be in a conflict situation with their bosses. When bosses disagree with them, Asian managers usually either avoid expressing what's on their mind or go along with what the bosses prefer. This is especially so when other people are present. Disagreeing with the boss publicly can be career-limiting.

It is important to recognize that the habit of "agreeing" with bosses no matter what carries with it grave consequences like the following:

- The boss will lose a valuable opportunity to hear useful insights from someone closer to the ground. Sensible bosses seek such input to help them stay relevant and be in touch with reality.
- By not speaking up, the manager becomes less effective in influencing events in the organization that he is in. He may even acquire the unenviable reputation of being a "yes-man." People around him will notice this.
- If there is no room for constructive conflict between the boss and her subordinate, the relationship is unlikely to be a mutually beneficial one. Resentment and suspicion will creep in. Soon such a contrived and oppressive relationship will pervade the rest of the company as well.
- Employee engagement will suffer. Today's workers want to be involved in decision-making. They also want a boss whom they can look up to.

Managers therefore find themselves caught between a rock and a hard place. They're damned if they do and damned if they don't. What steps can they take then?

First, observe the boss and understand how she typically responds to conflict. How does she handle conflicts with peers and her own boss? Know your own response mode too.

Second, talk to her privately to discuss how open she is to hear differing viewpoints. Does she prefer it done in private? Will she be comfortable hearing disagreement in public?

Third, err on the side of caution. Bring up disagreement in private and test her reaction. Find a comfortable way of raising the issue such as: "I do understand your viewpoint. May I offer another perspective on this, please?"

In fairness, there are many bosses who are enlightened and self-confident. They are keen to have regular sparring sessions with their colleagues. By getting to know them, you will find out about this. Why assume the worst?

Senior managers who are reading this have a big role to play as well if they want their subordinates to speak up. Broach the topic with each of them privately and, perhaps, publicly. Let people know that you are open for different perspectives. Then walk the talk. Don't shoot the first person who disagrees with you! You can unleash organization energy and create a more engaged workforce by being receptive to opposing views.

9. Make time to speak with your boss regularly
Know her work routine and agree on a mutually convenient time. Keep the sessions short and productive. It is useful to be on good terms with her secretary. She is the gatekeeper and can facilitate your accessibility to the boss.

10. Recognize that your boss holds your key to success
She knows things that you may not know. She can open doors for you. She can also better align your priorities to those of the company. Work well together and it will be a win-win for both of you.

- It is your responsibility to manage your relationship with your boss. Do it well, and you and your boss, as well as the company, will benefit.

- Know and apply the 10 steps in managing the boss-subordinate relationship.

Q1: How do you evaluate your current relationship with your boss?

Q2: What steps will you take to better manage it?

23 MANAGING OTHER STAKEHOLDERS

WHO ARE THE OTHER IMPORTANT STAKEHOLDERS?[1]

We have talked about your boss and your subordinates. Three other sets of important stakeholders will be your peers, customers and suppliers/business partners. You should also be aware of the potential challenges posed by former peers who are now your subordinates, disappointed rivals for your position and even your predecessor.

PEERS

In the first couple of weeks of your new position, reach out to your peers. Take the same approach as you have with your subordinates and your boss. Get to know each of them. Discuss each other's objectives and KPIs. Agree on how to help each other succeed.

Among peers, there will be certain relationships that will be especially important. These lie at the organizational fault lines. We explained this concept under conflict management. There will be plenty of opportunities for conflict to erupt because it would appear on the surface that your KPIs and those of your peers are mutually in opposition.

Devote more attention to cultivate trust and open dialogue with such peers. Together, you can reframe the situation that both of you are in. By collaborating with each other, both of you can meet your KPIs at the same time. Remember, this is not a zero sum game. You may also jointly approach each other's bosses to share with them how you intend to work together. I have seen bosses becoming pleasantly surprised by this new found spirit of collaboration. Perhaps, they should have initiated this themselves some time ago?

Some newly promoted managers find it awkward to relate to their new peers. These people were previously at a higher level and are indeed more experienced and older. Thus, the new managers continue to keep a discreet distance and remain deferential during meetings.

Be aware of this behaviour. This cannot be allowed to continue for too long. Otherwise, it would seem to peers that you are unsure of yourself. It's time to face up to this uncomfortable feeling. Start seeing these people as your peers.

Pluck up courage to have a one-on-one chat with them. Invite them for lunch, for example. Break the ice by saying that you're the new kid on the block and will have plenty of things to learn from them. Let them know that you do appreciate their guidance and help to settle into your new role. Many managers who take this approach tell me that they are encouraged by the support and understanding that their peers extend to them in return.

CUSTOMERS

If you have customers who you need to service, know who they are. Understand more about the relationship between your company and your key customers. Find more about the persons who you need to interface with on the customer side. Know what your predecessors have done in serving these customers. Then contact your key customers to introduce yourself and to understand how your company can continue to serve them, and to improve the relationship further. In the months ahead, deepen your relationship with your customers. Know more about their business model and seek to add greater value to them.

SUPPLIERS/BUSINESS PARTNERS

Connecting with your key suppliers/business partners is important as well. As with your customers, do some background work before inviting them to come and meet you. To get off on good footing, embrace the mindset that you would like to deal with your suppliers/business partners fairly. Remember the principle of reciprocity.

DISAPPOINTED RIVALS

Before you were appointed to your role, there could be a few other people who were in contention. One of them might even have been acting as the interim manager while management decided who would get the job. All these people, whether they admit it or not, must be disappointed that it's you and not they who became the manager.

Many new managers are so overwhelmed in their first few weeks or months that they unwittingly cold-shoulder such people. This can lead to troubles for the newcomer. For instance, your rival may resent your presence and not contribute during team meetings. While you try to excite your team, look around you and you may notice one or two persons who appear to be disengaged. Their disinterest may be contagious. There could be sympathy among other team members as well. See the managerial anecdote involving a new manager Kim in Chapter 8.

Again here, your EQ will be your best ally. Your IQ may have gained you your promotion but it is your EQ that will enable you to succeed in your new role. By tuning in to the dynamics around you, you can pick out quickly who you need to show greater care and attention to. Your boss may be able to alert you as well if you ask.

Take the initiative to speak to these persons directly. Don't wait for them to approach you. It will never happen. Show understanding for their disappointment. Create some space for them to adjust. Remember, it is not your fault that they didn't get the promotion, so don't apologize. Neither should you try to soothe them by making glib promises that you may not able to honour.

Exercise patience. Then discuss how you can work with each other for the future of the team. It's the job of the person to recover soon and be the performer that he is capable of becoming. Your job is to be fair to him and make him your ally.

BUDDIES AND PEERS WHO ARE NOW YOUR SUBORDINATES

This is another tricky relationship that must be managed, or else there will be a price to be paid.

Put yourself in the shoes of these people who have been your peers and buddies for many years. Not only had you and they worked in the trenches together, you had also played together—the lunches, dinners, the drinking sessions and weekend outings. Suddenly, they wake up to find that you're the boss. Their natural reaction is to be a little disoriented. There are a few questions that beg to be answered:

1. Now that you're the boss, what are your expectations of me?
2. It's getting complicated now. Do you wish to continue to be buddies or should we maintain some discreet distance?

Make no mistake about this. This can be a big challenge for the new manager and the buddies. Letting go of a relationship that has evolved over the years is tough. So what should you do?

By now, I expect that you know the drill. Take the initiative. You can either invite your buddies individually for a chat or meet as a group. You may talk over lunch. It's your call. Offering to stand treat is a good way to go. Expect some good-natured ribbing.

At the appropriate juncture, broach the topic of your relationship. They'll know what you mean. Ask them for their advice and perspective. Thank them for their friendship and support, and assure them that you continue to value their counsel and suggestions. They and you will have to get used to not being so chummy from now onwards. Some managers can't handle this, and want to continue to be great pals while being the boss. My advice is to learn to let go. Find new support groups among your new peers. This is the price of success, so to speak.

YOUR PREDECESSOR

The person who preceded you will continue to cast a shadow over your team whether you realize it or not. People will inevitably compare the new boss with the old one. The challenge will be further compounded if your predecessor has also been promoted and is still your boss, albeit another level up.

Spend some time discreetly understanding the differences between your predecessor and yourself in terms of working styles and priorities. As your people are used to working under the previous boss, there will be certain practices that they are wedded to. Ask yourself how important it is for you to change these. If it is not, it is better to let them continue. For areas that you prefer to change, explain clearly why.

If mistakes have been made by your predecessor, avoid finger-pointing and criticizing. Words will travel around. Instead, make the corrections and let the results speak for themselves. Over time, your people will adapt themselves to your leadership.

- As you settle in, know the key stakeholders that you will need to manage.

- Invest time to managing these key relations. It will make your assimilation into your new role a much smoother process.

Q1: How have you managed key relationships in your new role?

Q2: What do you need to do now?

24 MANAGING ORGANIZATIONAL POLITICS

WHAT IS ORGANIZATIONAL POLITICS?

Have you ever attended a meeting where there is something that many people will like to raise but nobody dares to do so? This is the elephant-in-the-room phenomenon. An elephant sitting in the room is so prominent that it's impossible for anyone to deny its existence. Yet, everybody pretends that it's not there.

So it is with organizational politics. We all see it and yet nobody dares to openly discuss it. The phrase conjures up images of back-stabbing, sabotaging, rumour-mongering and behind-the-scene manoeuvring. These are acts that no self-respecting professional will want to be associated with.

However, this is only one side of politics and what is commonly called destructive or dirty politics. There is yet another side to the coin: constructive politics. An expert on office politics puts it this way:

> *"To the successful executive in a competitive organization, day-to-day life is politics. There is no doubt that a high-level of field-based competence is needed to get ahead. But choose any two competent people, and the one who has political savvy, agility in the use of power and the ability to influence others will go further."*
> — *Kathleen Reardon*

It will help us have a more level-headed and meaningful discussion if we first agree on a definition of organization politics. Though there are many versions out there, I haven't found one that I feel is sufficiently balanced and neutral. This is how I'll define it:

Organizational politics is the art of influencing others towards a certain goal, and to enhance one's standing in the organization, through conventional and/or unconventional channels.

To help us gauge its appropriateness, we may attach two conditions:
- Is that "certain goal" in the company's interest or only self-interest?
- How fair, ethical and above board are the tactics used to influence?

Between "destructive" and "constructive" at the opposite poles of the spectrum, lie "apolitical", "politically naïve" and "lacking political savvy".

EXAMPLES OF POLITICAL SITUATIONS
Along the career highway, these are common sights that you may have observed or even encountered yourself.

Case 1: The politically naïve

This person focuses on getting his job done in the best possible way. He is reliable, focused, consistent and a strong team player. While others in the company will seek exposure to senior management, he shies away from the limelight. His philosophy is, "If you're good, people will know. I let my work speak for itself." Recently, when the company announced a promotion, he was passed over. Though he is disappointed, he rationalizes that the company knows the value he is bringing. His turn will come slowly but surely. Maybe next year.

Case 2: The politically savvy vs the apolitical

Two managers A and B are considered the hot favourites for a posting to the company's headquarters in New Jersey. It is generally understood that such a posting is a precursor for a higher position upon return to Asia. A and B are a study in opposites. While both are competent and highly regarded, A is much more outgoing and aggressive. He quickly finds out that the real decision-maker is a senior manager in New Jersey. He emails this person and sets up a series of calls to discuss his interest further. He also lobbies other managers who may be able to influence the final outcome. In contrast, B is less active and considers it odious to go around lobbying for support. He is aware that A is proactively "marketing" himself. However, he assumes that his boss will be able to speak up for him and leaves things basically to run their own course.

Case 3: Not everybody is completely above board

Senior management has just announced that due to budget constraints, a decision has to be made the following week on which of two projects to "kill." Tension is obviously running high as both project teams have worked long and hard. While the two teams are burning the midnight oil to justify funding for themselves, the leader of one of the teams decides to do more than just that. Among the senior managers who will make the final call next week is someone he knows since their days back in the university. He plans to invite him for a dinner this weekend. Apart from seeking his support for his project, he has a few insights on why the other project is not worth spending another cent on, and he is more than ready to share them.

Case 4: The manager who can't connect emotionally
June is feeling very dejected. For the life of her, she just can't figure out why her opinions don't receive a fair hearing. She's convinced that they are technically sound and well-thought out. Yet time after time, all she gets is a polite nod from her colleagues and the bosses. She has tried to seek input on how she can get people's attention when she speaks. They all say the same thing *ad nauseam*: "You are not relating to us on the same emotional plane. Each time you speak, the flow of ideas is disrupted. It's like you have hijacked our high-speed car for a detour. You also overwhelm us with so much detail that we all lose the plot."

HOW TO BE POLITICALLY SAVVY

I have debated long and hard with myself on how much I should share in this chapter on organizational politics. This being a book for first-time managers, will I not be unnecessarily alarming the readers? Perhaps, I should just leave this out as it's unlikely that there will be that much politicking at this level?

Friends who have read the draft of this book are split on this question. As it is left to me as the author, I weigh in with those who advise, "Forewarned is forearmed."

Politics is not a spectator sport. You can't sit there and watch for it to be played out on someone else's territory. There is a strange characteristic about politics. It seeks out those who are least interested in it. When it hits you, there will be severe repercussions on your career. And as you have seen in the earlier examples, you need not be at the senior rungs of management to be afflicted.

Whenever people interact, politics is the natural by-product. Ignoring it, or being apolitical, is not an option. The only way to ignore it is to seek a job in a remote location where you don't need to interact with people. That of course means short-changing and marginalizing yourself, while more politically astute colleagues stride ahead to take on bigger roles and become more influential. Being politically naïve or lacking political savvy will lead to the same fate.

On the other hand, if you complement your professional competence with political skills, you will become more effective in advancing your career and the interests of your organization. The politics that we are advocating here is constructive politics which we can define as *"the art of influencing others towards a course of action that will advance the shared goals of the individuals involved as well as those of the organization."*

Developing political savvy is not an overnight exercise. It will take awareness, interest and application over the course of your career. The sooner you get started, the better in control of your career trajectory you will be.

Albert Einstein was once asked: "Dr. Einstein, why is it that when the mind of man has stretched so far to discover the structure of the atom we have been unable to devise the political means to keep the atom from destroying us?"[1]

The great scientist replied, "This is simple, my friend. It is because politics is more difficult than physics."

The foundation for political savvy is EQ. The outcome is to be able to influence others effectively by shrewd management of key relationships. Here is a framework to help you develop greater political savvy.

Step 1: Establish a sound track record
This is the most fundamental requirement. Know what you are required to do. Get your priorities right and spend your time wisely. Do such a great job that you excel in achieving all the goals assigned to you.

Step 2: Build a good reputation
Be aware that people who work with you are constantly observing

you and others. What is that image you would like others to have of you? For instance, you would like people to view you this way: "I'm seen as trustworthy, reliable, having no hidden agenda, capable and well-regarded. When I'm faced with tough challenges, I do not cave in. I will collaborate with others and come up with a creative solution that is a win-win for all involved."

Work hard to build this image for yourself. While it is better to let action speak louder than words, do not pass up on opportunities to let bosses know of the achievements you and your team have accomplished. Do it professionally and appropriately. Have a point of view on key issues and be prepared to speak up in meetings.

Step 3: Build alliances
Know who the powerful people are. Often, your immediate boss is the first person whose support you need. Frequently, it may not be enough. You may need to be on the good side of your boss's boss and other senior people.

Win the support and respect of your peers and subordinates as well. Leverage the principle of reciprocity. Think win-win and seek to collaborate. Build up a healthy emotional bank account with all you work with. You may need to draw upon them sometime in the future.

Step 4: Develop and fine-tune your political awareness
Take interest in what is going on in your environment. Train yourself to spot shifting trends and clues that emanate when people around you interact, especially the senior managers. This is not to suggest that you devote your time like a corporate Sherlock Holmes sniffing things out. Far from it, in line with Step 1, your main focus is to do your job. While doing it, remember to look up regularly and scan the environment. Take little at face value. You may be able to take in cues that others miss. Pay attention to what your intuition is telling you.

Step 5: Work on your influencing skills
Be familiar with the eight levers of influence we'd discussed earlier. Know when and how to use them in various situations and with stakeholders.

Step 6: Think on your feet
Watch how successful leaders field and respond to questions. What do you do when others raise questions that you have no answers to? What if people don't buy your idea? Get out of your comfort zone and get some real-life practices out there during meetings. Practice makes perfect.

Step 7: Pick your battles
Remember the adage, "You can win a battle and still lose the war?" Not every battle is worth winning. Occasionally, it is better to let others win. You also don't need to have the last word. That said, be aware that sometimes you need to make a stand and win. For instance, if a colleague is spreading half-truths and disinformation about you and your team, it is time to respond forcefully. Get your facts right and muster your resources. Then act decisively and straighten him out. It is unlikely that the person will dare repeat this act of aggression on you after this.

Even as you deal with this particular incident, remember it is still possible to be both firm and magnanimous when making your point. This quote may be a fitting close for this chapter.

"Provide your adversaries a footpath along which they can retreat."
— Sun Tzu in *The Art of War*

- Whenever people interact, politics is the natural by-product. Ignoring it is not an option. Those who do so will find themselves marginalized.

- Only by complementing your professional competence with political savvy will you be able to advance your career and the interests of your organization.

Q1: What examples of organizational politics have you personally encountered recently?

Q2: How did you handle them then? How will you handle them now?

PART SIX
Becoming A More Complete Leader

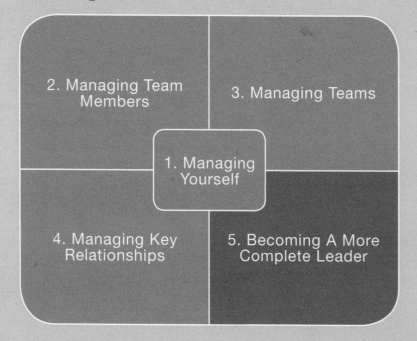

2. Managing Team Members

3. Managing Teams

1. Managing Yourself

4. Managing Key Relationships

5. Becoming A More Complete Leader

*"We shall not cease from exploring and the
end of our exploring will be to arrive where we started
and know the place for the first time."*
—T.S. Eliot

25 THE IMPORTANCE OF SELF-RENEWAL

WHY YOU NEED TO RECHARGE YOURSELF

In the introduction to this book, I promised to provide you a telescope as you embark on your journey as a manager. In this and the last chapter, you will get two peeks into the telescope. The first one concerns your well-being, while the second look shows you the long runway in your career trajectory.

As a first-time manager, you will have many more milestones ahead of you. Hopefully, with each signpost that you come to, you will find new meaning, purpose and sense of satisfaction. One thing you can count on is that on the road to corporate success, you will be putting in long hours which will take a toll on you physically, mentally and emotionally.

Going by the war stories of "successful people" before us, a common pattern emerges: An endless series of 12 to 14-hour workdays, mounting workload, exhaustion, little family time, constant travelling, poor sleeping habits, unhealthy meals, no time for exercise and weight gain.

The human body, wonderfully resilient and robust as it is, can go on and on taking a lot of abuse and punishment, all in the service of its owners—us. But one day, it will stop working. And that can come suddenly, as the examples that I shall be sharing will show.

If we want to be able to bring more of ourselves to work and live to a ripe old age, then we must invest in our well-being. This means inculcating the ritual of renewing ourselves regularly. There are four domains involved: physical, mental, emotional and spiritual.

The key is to build into our daily routine short breaks so that we can disengage and recharge ourselves before jumping into the fray again. A manager who has a sense of well-being brings positive energy, hope and optimism to the workplace. He is living a life that will be an inspiration for others to emulate.

IS WORK-LIFE BALANCE ATTAINABLE?

The concept of work-life balance has not gained much traction in Asia. Though many governments are alarmed by the falling fertility rates in their population and are actively promoting family-friendly policies, people here tend to put work above everything else.

This work ethic has enabled many Asian countries to make up for lost time and to catch up economically with the developed parts of the world. It also gives Asia a competitive edge over more developed Western countries.

For what it's worth, it is useful at this point for the first-time manager to pause and address a fundamental question: "Should this be the modus operandi for me for the rest of my career?"

Underpinning this question are two assumptions:

Assumption 1: It is hard work and long hours that have made us successful. If we cut back on these, we'll become soft and will lose out.

Assumption 2: Look at what is happening to the Western countries. While they enjoy a higher quality of life, they are also paying a price in declining economic vigour. Do we want to be like them?

This is the zero-sum argument. Sounds much like the "either-or" mindset, doesn't it? Based on this, between work and life, work must always come first. Perhaps, even second, third and fourth. So where does it leave life? Far be it for me to suggest that workers in Asia should abandon their ethic of hard work. However, work and life need not be mutually exclusive. As Asian workers move up the economic ladder and become exposed to new ideas and best practices from around the world, it behooves us to challenge age-old practices and test new possibilities.

We need not continue to accept as an article of faith that the only way to stay ahead is to let work be our be-all and end-all. This is what the Boomers have been doing for the last three to four decades. And one day, they wake up and realize that life has passed them by while they were going full tilt to earn a living.

We have previously discussed the concept of balancing between two polar opposites. The linear "either-or" paradigm accepts unquestioningly that it is either work or life we have to choose between. Hence we choose work. Let's reconsider. We need not be imprisoned by this outmoded thinking. Let's instead invoke the concept of complementarity as in the Eastern philosophy of Yin Yang.

All of a sudden, work-life balance does sound plausible, doesn't it? Well, life is not a spectator sport. It is up to each and every one of us to test this hypothesis and strive for the work-life balance that we seek. It's a call that each of us must make to decide what works for us. Let's look at how one manager does it in the following anecdote.

Managerial Anecdote

George was a young, high-flying manager in his company. His working hours were so extreme that his bosses became alarmed and were convinced that he was heading towards a complete breakdown. Typically, he would be in the office at 7 a.m. and he wouldn't leave earlier than 9 p.m., working non-stop and even skipping lunch. Back at home, he would take a quick bath, wolf down some food and then continue working on his computer until 1 a.m. He would take phone calls from the European offices as well.

As he rose early for work and returned home late, his two young children had no interaction with him at all on weekdays. His wife was feeling neglected as George had absolutely no time for her.

On weekends, it was only slightly better. Though George made it a point to spend time with the children, he was otherwise constantly preoccupied with work. As his children put it, Dad was always working, working and working.

When I met George at his boss's request, sitting in front of me was a nervous and highly- strung young man. At just 34 years old, he was already the Chief Financial Officer or CFO of the European company in Asia. In the last 18 months he had either been travelling or working nearly 24/7 throughout. By his own admission, he wouldn't be able to last long. He even shared the story of another senior executive in the company who worked just like he. One day, this person woke up and found himself half-paralyzed. With a wry smile, George said he hoped he wouldn't end up like this.

In the days ahead, he arranged for me to speak with his bosses, peers and subordinates one-on-one to seek their perspectives on his leadership style and working patterns. I also requested to meet with his wife.

What emerged from the interviews was a fascinating picture of a talented person who had lost his sense of balance. He used to be an avid outdoor person who looked forward to his weekends with his family and friends. All that changed when he was quickly promoted many rungs up the ladder. His rapid ascent exceeded his wildest imagination. He was both gratified by the recognition accorded by his bosses and overwhelmed by his increasingly heavy responsibilities.

Co-workers described a kindly and approachable leader who put others' interest ahead of his own. He was always available for his people—the financial controllers in the countries. Many felt that he was doing work which should have been delegated to them. As he would never say no, colleagues in Europe would make "outrageous requests" for financial data from him. If they wanted them overnight, he would oblige and do it himself.

In the months ahead, George started to understand that the long, punishing hours that he was pulling were in a large part his own doing: not delegating; doing what his subordinates should rightfully be doing; being overly accommodating; not pushing back when he should have, and more importantly, not stepping up to his new responsibilities as a CFO. He also now understood for the first time that his financial controllers, all of whom were senior people, felt that he wasn't trusting and empowering them. A few put it quite bluntly, "Let us do our job. We are experienced and perfectly capable. We don't need him to come to our countries to handhold us!"

Three months later, George regained his balance and reclaimed his life. Each morning, he would start the day at 6 a.m. with a 30-minute jog or swim. He would arrive at the office at 7.30 a.m. and leave latest at 7 p.m. By the time he got home, the kids would still be awake. Once the children were in bed, he would work till 9 p.m. After that, as agreed with his wife, he would turn off his computer and his BlackBerry, and devote full attention to her.

He delegated more and empowered his people. Trips to the various countries were reduced from weekly events to travelling on a need-to basis. As he described it, "There is not much need to travel. My guys are on top of the situation. We can check in through emails or over the phone."

George had learnt to push back and say no to "outrageous requests". Weekends were now for the family. Working hours had reduced drastically and work and life were now in greater balance. He had become less stressed and more calm. Productivity had improved significantly.

He also discovered that as a senior leader, the way he managed his work-life had an impact on other people around him, for better or for worse. Months ago, when he was spinning out of control, the same feeling was transmitted to his people. They became just as stressed. Now, with his new found balance, the climate had perked up considerably. Colleagues were happier and the mood became one of optimism. Such was the power of emotional contagion. A cheerful heart radiates positive energy that can be picked up by the people around you.

STRESS MANAGEMENT

It is commonly understood that a certain amount of stress is necessary for optimal performance. However, too much stress over a prolonged period of time can be extremely harmful. Not only will the people afflicted burn out, their judgment will become erratic. Workplace tension will rise as colleagues become more snappy and short-fused.

When people are constantly under stress and running around frantically, productivity will nosedive. They will work harder and longer and make more errors. Just like the hamster running on the wheel.

Latest studies[1] have shown that stress does not just grip us and let go. It will change us by altering our bodies and our brains. When we are stressed, our bodies are flooded with a surge of bio-chemicals. This onslaught chips away at our immune systems, paving the way to cancer, infection and disease. Hormones unleashed by stress eat at our digestive tract and lungs, causing ulcers and asthma. They may also attack the heart, leading to strokes and heart disease. In short, chronic stress is like a slow poison. It kills.

To counter stress, we need to build into our daily routine some anti-stress techniques. Here are some of the keys ones you may enjoy. You will have to experiment and find out what works for you.

- Physical exercises such as jogging, walking, swimming, tennis
- Meditation
- The relaxation response first described by Harvard's Dr. Herbert Benson
- Doing tai-chi or yoga
- Listening to music
- Hanging out with the family
- Playing with children, walking the dog, etc

ARE YOU GETTING SUFFICIENT SLEEP?

Many hard-charging managers pride themselves on their ability to work long hours with very little sleep. Like George in our anecdote, such people think that all they need is about four hours, or even less, of sleep. This is a dangerous fallacy. Chronic sleep deficit is not only a performance killer but may cause death!

Recently, I read an article in *The Times of India* reporting the death of Ranjan Das, CEO and Managing Director of SAP for

India. Mr. Das was 42 and the youngest CEO of a multinational corporation in the country. He had just returned after working out in a gym when he collapsed and died of a heart attack.

According to SAP sources, Das epitomized hard work, integrity and a sense of curiosity. He led a very healthy lifestyle, eating right and jogging daily. He had no bad habits such as drinking or smoking, and was always a bundle of energy. Only a few months previously he had even run the Chennai marathon. He was so ambitious and driven that he allowed himself only four hours of sleep a day.

I too had my personal wake-up call a few years ago. In fact, it took two calls to get my attention. At one stage, my consultancy work was so busy that I survived on less than five hours of sleep each day. I was working round the clock, seven days a week, and travelling extensively.

Though my back was constantly in pain and I was suffering from migraine, I ignored all the warning signs and plugged on. Then my body decided to rebel. I suffered a seizure at 8 p.m. at home one night while awaiting a teleconference with my counterparts in Europe. Though I was bedridden for four days, the message was lost on me. As soon as I was out of the hospital, I was back to my punishing routine. Ten months later, I had a second fit—a massive one this time. According to family members and paramedics who arrived, I was in convulsion for an hour while people around me looked on helplessly.

I was placed in intensive care for nearly 10 days. On the night of my admission to the hospital, the doctors warned my family members to prepare for the worst. They said my condition was so bad that it was unlikely that I would pull through. I was put on drip and a life-support system. My life was hanging by a thread. I did pull through. Now the message has finally sunk in.

Our brains need on the average about seven to eight hours of sleep every night. It is foolish, and indeed, dangerous to deprive ourselves of sleep. Not only is chronic sleep deficit a performance killer, it may kill the performer as well.

- Make your own well-being a priority in your life. It's not a good-to-have; it is a must-have. Encourage your people to do the same.

- Build in regular breaks into your daily routine to renew yourself.

Q1: How have you been managing your well-being?

Q2: What self-renewal strategies will you adopt?

HOW ARE YOU DOING SO FAR AS A MANAGER?

In the transition programmes that I conduct for first-time managers, I emphasize that learning to lead requires hard work and dedication. It is not a classroom activity where you intellectualize what you plan to do. The real learning will take place at the workplace when you interact with co-workers on a day-to-day basis, tackling real-life challenges. It involves a shift in certain leadership behaviours and will not occur overnight. Sometimes it takes months. At times, it will take longer.

This is the last chapter of this book. I congratulate you for staying the course with me. It is timely to pause and check how you are progressing. How will you respond to the following questions:

1. How far have you progressed in putting in place the five foundation stones for first-time managers? Check against the KSIs suggested.
2. What changes have you noticed in yourself?
3. What is the single most important thing that you have learnt about being a leader?
4. How do you define the values that are appropriate to your level?

The transition programmes which I conduct are done in two modules spread out over six to ten months. All participants are required to identify two or three leadership behaviours that they would like to develop further. They do these after receiving input from bosses and co-workers. At the end of the programme, we would conduct an online survey to solicit input from bosses, peers and co-workers on what progress, if any, has been observed in the leadership behaviours identified.

These are the general observations:
- The survey results show that most participants will have indeed made progress. There will be a minority, though, who are assessed as showing little progress.
- Those deemed to have the most noticeable progress have applied themselves consistently at the workplace. Additionally, they have approached co-workers, thanked them for providing preworkshop input and shared what they intend to work on. Co-workers are generally appreciative of such openness and become sensitized to their development effort. Such participants are unconsciously leading by example and sowing the seeds for a learning climate in the organizations.
- When bosses take an active interest in the development of the participants, the latter show even greater progress.
- Participants who have become much more self-aware, and who know that before they can change others, they have to first change themselves, are more impactful as leaders. Anecdotally, I notice that they are more versatile and adaptable. They also move upwards much faster.

As you continue your leadership journey, let's take a quick peek into what the future may hold. I would like to leave you with two parting thoughts.

REMEMBER TO LEARN, UNLEARN AND RELEARN

As you ascend the corporate ladder in the years ahead, there will be greater responsibilities and challenges. New skills and mindset will be required. You will need to manage more complex relationships. The higher you go, the more you need to be visionary and strategic. And at the same time, you have to be in touch with people lower in the organization whose responsibilities are much more operational and "here-and-now".

Be prepared to make learning, unlearning and relearning a

lifelong habit. Develop interest in an eclectic range of subjects. Read widely, both fiction and non-fiction. Talk to people in realms of experience completely different from yours. Travel widely and learn from people from all walks of life. Take frequent pauses to reflect and to decide what to do next. Recognize that jobs and occupations are going to be transitory. Don't count on lifelong employment with one organization. The future belongs to those who are able to reinvent themselves every few years.

Proficiency in both spoken and written English is a prerequisite for business success. It therefore pays to improve one's command of the English language. For Westerners in Asia, find out more about Eastern culture, and learn to speak some basic Mandarin.

MAKE REFLECTION A HABIT

Saying that one should never stop learning has become a cliché. What is the purpose of learning? If two persons possess similar learning, what will put one apart from the other?

Russell Ackoff, a systems theorist and professor of organizational change, has developed a useful way to understand how we can progress up the hierarchy of knowledge towards wisdom. His views are represented by the DIKW Pyramid. What transforms one level in the hierarchy to the higher one until ultimately it becomes wisdom, is reflection.

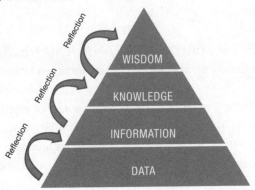

The DIKW Pyramid

"By three methods we may learn wisdom. First by reflection, which is noblest. Second, by imitation, which is easiest. Third, by experience which is bitterest."

— Confucius

DISCOVER A SECOND PASSION[1]

It is an unspoken but well accepted ethos that has served us well since time immemorial. Find an area of specialization and devote your life to it. This will bring you a lifetime of success and security. Thus we see people at an early age deciding to specialize as engineers, accountants, lawyers, doctors or musicians. The choices we make in our youthful days will define our careers and shape our lives.

Being a Boomer, this was the path that I took as I knew of no other way then. My choice of specialization was engineering. A few years into my working life while in my late twenties, my vista and perspective expanded somewhat. I started to discover new interests and possibilities. Suddenly remaining as an engineer didn't seem such a cool idea. The notion of becoming a corporate honcho, running a business with full P&L (profit & loss) responsibilities soon become my all-consuming passion. I did attain that and was enjoying much satisfaction in running the Asia-Pacific operations for a multinational corporation. Then in my early forties, I woke up one day and found that something was missing. The passion had gone. It was then that I cast my eyes around and soon discovered my "second passion"—working with leaders in organizations to help them become better leaders.

In a way, this didn't come as a surprise. As I recall it, even as far back as a teenager, I was interested in studying human behaviour. An incident in my university days remains etched in my memory. One day, not far from a dreaded exam on thermodynamics in my third year in engineering, all my classmates were feverishly mugging away. I, on the other hand, was wasting my time immersed at one end of the library reading a *Harvard Business Review* article.

A few well-meaning friends expressed surprise at my poor use of study time. One person, however, said something prescient, "One day, you will probably find yourself doing something very different from engineering."

And so it came to pass. In my early forties, I left corporate life and set up my own consultancy in leadership development. It has been more than 12 years and I'm still at it. Each day, I wake up feeling a spring in my step. This is my second passion in my career journey.

Whatever profession you have chosen, there will be much to learn in the years ahead. However, be open and receptive to other interests that you may develop along the way. Go beyond just work and family life. Take an active interest in your community.

Look around you. You may see examples of eminent people who have had a number of successful career changes. Some of these people may be meaningfully engaged in their day job as academics, bankers or doctors while actively pursuing an interest as a musician, painter or photographer and helping out in the community in their spare time. Then at a later stage in their lives, they decide to devote full time to their second passion.

Nobody says you shouldn't specialize. But don't let your choice of specialization ring-fence the rest of your life. You may have more to offer people around you. By exploring wider and deeper, I'm sure you will find greater fulfilment.

- Learn, unlearn and relearn. Reinvent yourself every few years.
- Discover, develop and pursue an outside interest. It may be your second passion.

Q1: What would you like to do 10 years from now?

Q2: How do you intend to get there?

Appendices

APPENDIX ONE:
A COACHING CONVERSATION[1]

Cheng is the Marketing Manager. Lucy is a product specialist reporting to him. She started as a management trainee fresh from the university. Within 18 months she has shown herself to be a cut above her cohort. She is ambitious and impatient for larger responsibilities, and has demonstrated great self-confidence and the ability to work with little supervision.

Cheng is impressed and feels that she will be ready to be a product manager soon. He has one area of concern though. She's so hard-driving that she tends to be quite ruthless in pursuing her goals. Unless she learns to be more sensitive towards her co-workers, she will risk alienating people around her. As her manager, he feels that it is his responsibility to help her smooth out her rough edges.

A new product in the Gerome men's skincare range will be launched soon, and Cheng has decided that he will assign it to Lucy to manage. She is delighted at Cheng's confidence in her as she knows that a product launch is usually handled by more experienced and senior staff. Cheng has also assigned a management trainee, Amy to help Lucy.

It has been two months. Only yesterday, Cheng heard that Lucy has had a big argument with the Supply Chain team on some stock issues for the launch. It has also come to his attention that friction has developed between Lucy and the advertising agency. Cheng knows he has to speak to Lucy urgently. He picks up the phone and arranges for her to come to his office that afternoon for a chat.

Cheng: *Yo, Lucy. Come on in.*

Lucy: *Hi, Cheng. What's up?*

Cheng: *It's just to catch up with you on the Gerome launch. Can we have a short discussion on your progress?*

Lucy:	Sure. No problem.
Cheng:	Great. How's the preparation coming along?
Lucy:	Still on schedule. The launch will take place as you know in about three months' time. Most of the logistics should be ready by then.
Cheng:	Please tell me a little more.

Pause. Lucy looks a little hesitant. Cheng remains silent and gives her the space to organize her thoughts.

Lucy:	The logistics are moving according to the timeline as discussed with you. There are only two areas that I am a little concerned about.
Cheng:	What are they?
Lucy:	The Supply Chain people may have some difficulty getting us the stocks in time for the launch. The other worrying thing is that all the advertisements may not be ready by then.
Cheng:	Apart from these two items, is there anything else that I should know?
Lucy:	No, only these two items.
Cheng:	What is the status on these two items?
Lucy:	Yesterday, I spoke to Johnny the Supply Chain Manager. He told me that my stocks for the launch may be delayed because I did not give him sufficient lead time.
Cheng:	When must they arrive?
Lucy:	Latest in eight weeks' time. I was really upset because he only mentioned this to me now. It's not my fault.
Cheng:	How did you resolve this with Johnny?
Lucy:	We did not come to any agreement. It was quite nasty. We both pointed fingers at each other.

Lucy looks very distressed. There is a long pause. Then, she continues.

Lucy: *If only I had remained cool and not yelled at him.*

Cheng: *Sounds like there was a blow-up between the two of you. What do you need to straighten out now?*

Lucy: *We must get the stocks here in time for the launch. We need at least eight weeks in order for us to get the channels ready. Cheng, can you please step in here and apply some pressure on Johnny? This will be a show-stopper. And if it happens, it's the fault of the Supply Chain Team.*

Cheng: *I can tell that you are upset. You're right, it will be a show-stopper if the stocks don't arrive in time. Lucy, if you recall, you assured me that you will be able to handle this launch. So is this a "go" or "no go" now?*

Silence. Lucy is deep in thought. Then she speaks up with renewed vigour.

Lucy: *Cheng, please don't worry. I will make it a success.*

Cheng: *I'm glad to hear this. What must you do to get the stocks here in time?*

Lucy: *Immediately after this, I'll go and sit down with Johnny. The first thing I should do is to apologize to him for being so hot-headed. I'm sure if we work with each other, we can sort this out.*

Cheng: *That's a good approach. When can you let me know the outcome of your discussions with Johnny?*

Lucy: *I'll call you on your mobile phone. I know you will be out with customers this afternoon.*

Cheng: *Sound good. What about the advertisement?*

Lucy: *There are quite a few changes that I made last week. The advertising agency is telling me that I must stop making so many changes to the artwork. Otherwise, the ads will not be ready. Actually, I think this is poor attitude on their part. They're very inflexible! We are their customers. They should accommodate all our needs. Aren't customers always right?*

Cheng: *What's behind all these changes?*

A long pause. Silence.

Lucy: *I guess I'm just too overwhelmed with work. There are many details that are incorrect, so I'm trying to amend them.*

Cheng: *It is very important for you to understand that our advertising agency is one of our closest partners. We need to treat them as we treat our internal people. Put yourself in their shoes. How will you be affected by these last minute changes?*

Lucy: *I see what you mean. They have their own internal processes and will need time. I guess I'll be very frustrated as well. Cheng, I don't want my ads to be delayed. I'll be more careful from now on.*

Cheng: *What about your management trainee, Amy? How is she helping you?*

Lucy: *Frankly, she's too new. I have not involved her at all.*

Cheng: *What does she do then?*

Lucy: *Nothing much. She doesn't know about our culture. I'll brief her after the launch.*

Cheng: *Lucy, look at your career path. You came in as a*

> *management trainee 18 months ago. Today, you are able to handle a product launch on your own. What has contributed to the fast pace of your development?*

There is a long silence. Lucy seems puzzled. Then, a slight smile appears on her face.

Lucy: *I was lucky. You got me involved from Day One. Though I started from ground zero, you had faith in me and allowed me to take on one task after another. That's how I learned. You're right. I must involve Amy. I can't do everything on my own. I will start by having her work with the advertising agency. That will be good training for her. I'll do the final checking.*

Cheng: *I think we are making good progress here. Still, there is quite a bit of work for you to follow up on. Shall we meet again soon? To nail things down?*

Lucy: *Yes. Thanks for spending time with me. I'm aware that this product launch is crucial. I will work with Johnny and Amy on the remaining two critical items. Shall we meet on Monday? I will give you the latest update then.*

Notes

In this scenario, Manager Cheng first diagnoses the developmental needs of his subordinate Lucy and then assigns her a project that will facilitate her growth. He follows up closely and coaches her.

In the coaching conversation, the GROW process is used. Are you able to identify the four stages: Goal, Reality, Options and Way Forward? Notice the use of probing and open-ended questions. At various junctures, Cheng stays cool and allows silence to nudge Lucy along.

Lucy first tries to blame others for what is happening. She then attempts to put the monkey on her manager's back. She also has not been able to delegate, thereby over burdening herself and making a series of mistakes. Her boss recognizes all these and is able to shift her perspective and have her take accountability for making the product launch a success. Also notice how the conversation is conducted in a calm and composed manner.

Admittedly, for people who have tried coaching subordinates, this conversation seems too easy. This role-play is meant to illustrate how the GROW process and coaching proficiencies may be utilised. When you conduct coaching, do expect some resistance. It is unlikely it will proceed as smoothly as in this instance.

APPENDIX TWO: HOW BOSSES CAN FACILITATE SUCCESSFUL TRANSITION FOR FIRST-TIME MANAGERS

Becoming a manager for the first-time is both exciting, rewarding and traumatic. As this book has shown, the process of developing into a manager is not a linear one. A person who has performed very well as a specialist or an individual contributor does not intuitively morph into a manager.

There is first a need to understand that they need to perform a different role and add values appropriate to their level. In order to do this, they need to take on a new identity, acquire new skills and do less of what has made them successful previously. The transformation can be quite complex and difficult.

Bosses can facilitate their successful transition by taking the following steps:

1. Partner with their learning and development organization to organize a transition programme for first-time managers.

2. Devote time one-on-one to facilitate the on-boarding for these managers. Discuss the shifts that they will have to make as they step into their new roles. Help them understand how their success will be defined. What values do you expect from them as managers? See the "Leadership Turns Framework"[1] in Appendix Four. It will be very useful if you could work through the framework with the new managers. You can hasten their learning by sharing your own learning experiences in adjusting to managerial responsibilities.

3. New managers, and even experienced managers, struggle with balancing between results-focus and people-focus. The mindset is that it is either one or the other. Not both. Help them make a paradigm shift. Effective managers do not settle for either. They want both. Consider replacing KPIs with KSIs (See Chapters 2 and 4). And nothing speaks more compellingly than having you show them the way.

4. Demonstrate a real and abiding interest in their growth. Have a discussion on their strengths and areas for development. Coach them and provide constructive feedback regularly. Provide input to their PDP or Personal Development Plan (See Chapter 6).

5. Be patient. Cut them some slack by providing some room for learning from their mistakes.

6. Remember your subordinates will see you as a role model. Be the manager that you want them to be.

APPENDIX THREE: LEVERAGING HUMAN CAPITAL FOR SUSTAINABLE COMPETITIVE ADVANTAGE

Practitioners in learning and development have much to contribute to organizations in the 21st century. Through the human capital strategy, they can powerfully impact business performance by addressing four areas that we have touched on in this book and thereby enhance competitive advantage on a sustainable basis.

1. Facilitating transition for first-time managers

Many of the world's leading multinational corporations have recognized the importance of managerial transitions. Indeed as explained earlier in this book, the transition into first-time management is pivotal and foundational. How well new managers make this turn will determine not only their effectiveness as a manager now, but will also influence the way they lead in the future as they become senior leaders.

Companies which do an excellent job in transitioning their first-time managers take the following approach:

- Enroll new managers into a transition programme either just before or after they embark on their new responsibilities.

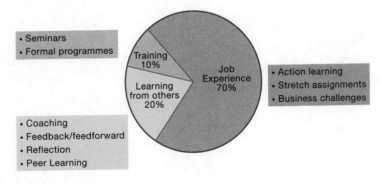

Diagram A3: 70-20-10 principle

- Adopt the 70-20-10 principle[1] (Refer to Diagram A3). In leadership development, people learn best through job experiences (70 percent) reinforced by learning from others (20 percent) and training (10 percent).
- Involve the participants' managers in the transition programme. Indeed they are key to its success.

2. Educate managers about the concept of going up the value chain
Leaders at all levels in organizations need to deliver the values appropriate to their respective levels. This is largely unrecognized and poorly understood in many organizations, both in the private and public sectors around the world. In the words of Charan, Drotter and Noel, authors of *The Leadership Pipeline: How to build the Leadership Powered Company*, "In some companies, at least 50 percent of people in leadership positions are operating far below their assigned layer. They have the potential..., but that potential is going unfulfilled. In short, they're stuck and clogging up the system." In other words, they are destroying values.

Corporations are now asking, "How do we ensure that at every level in our organization, each manager is a value creator?"

To tip the balance in their favour, such companies organize transition programmes to prepare for different levels of responsibilities. Typically, beyond transition to first-time management, the next two programmes will be to middle management and to senior management respectively.

By adopting the "Leadership Turns Framework" in Appendix Four, they educate their managers about the concept of going up the value chain throughout the organization.

3. Extracting synergy and value through teamwork
Although we, in this networked economy, have all recognized that teams are the central vehicle for getting complex activities done, organizations generally struggle with creating high-performance teams. Though leaders will routinely and ritualistically bring

people together and slap the label of TEAM on them, in truth, a huge proportion of teams are under-performing at all levels in organizations. Even at the executive level—the Chief Executive Officer (CEO) and his direct reports.

Under-performing teams can be a huge drain on the physical and emotional health of the people involved. The ramifications are wider and even more far-reaching if it's the senior leadership team that is dysfunctional.

Building high-performance teams is a key source of competitive advantage. Companies which do this successfully will be streets ahead of others in their business space. See Part Four of this book.

4. Raise employees' engagement level
As mentioned in Chapter 17, the majority of employees are unengaged. Only one out of five workers is engaged. Two out of five are waiting to be engaged. The remaining two have checked out in one form or another. The contributing factors: organizational leadership, work environment, career growth and care of employees as individuals. Imagine the impact on the company's performance if three out of five employees become engaged.

Looking at the four areas above, there is one common denominator—leadership.

Remember: In organizations,
everything rises and falls on leadership.

A significant step forward will be to hold leaders accountable not only for delivering the "what" but also the "how". Consider replacing KPIs with KSIs. See Chapters 2 and 4.

APPENDIX FOUR:
LEADERSHIP TURNS FRAMEWORK

FACTORS	SPECIALIST	FIRST-LINE MANAGER
(a) Key Responsibilities	1. 2. 3. 4. 5.	1. 2. 3. 4. 5.
(b) Key Skills	1. 2. 3. 4. 5.	1. 2. 3. 4. 5.
(c) Key Stakeholders		
(d) Value-added		

The principle here is that as we move up the organization, our value added at the higher position is fundamentally different from, and greater than, that at the previous position. This is the challenge of making a leadership turn. By doing this analysis, we can see immediately the vital differences between different management levels. By and large, these are the various positions of ascending responsibilities in an organization: (a) Specialist, (b) Section Manager, (c) Department Manager, (d) Director/Senior Director, (e) Vice President/General Manager, (f) President.

Separate exercises may need to be done as follows: (a) to (b), (b) to (c), (c) to (d), (d) to (e), and (e) to (f).

There are four dimensions in making a successful transition. They are as follows:

(a) Key Responsibilities: What are the top four to five key responsibilities here? These should account for 80 percent of the requirements of the job at this level.

(b) Key Skills: What new skills, hard and soft, should be developed and acquired? How will you get them?

(c) Key Stakeholders: The higher one goes, the more complex one's relationship with other stakeholders and constituencies gets. Managing relationship with these stakeholders will be a key determinant of success.

(d) Value-added: What are the critical deliverables that are appropriate to this level?

Litmus Test: After you complete the framework for the positions of Specialist and First-Line Manager, do you see significant differences between these two positions? Marginal differences may be due to two factors: (a) the managerial role is insufficiently understood or (b) the analysis has not been sufficiently thorough.

ENDNOTES

In writing this book, I have drawn upon the lessons and experience gathered from numerous assignments and programmes with various clients over the last decade. I have also made references to many books and articles that have been of great help for me in my 30-odd years in business management and consultancy.

Many sources have already been acknowledged in the book. In the following notes, I have indicated other sources that correspond with statements, phrases or ideas, that appear in specific chapters of the book.

Introduction
1. Maitland, A. "Top Women Tip the Scales," *Financial Times*, (Oct 11, 2007).

Chapter 1: Are you ready to play a bigger game?
1. Hill, L. *Becoming A Manager: How New Managers Master the Challenges of Leadership*. (Boston, Harvard Business School Press, 2003).
2. Charan, R., Drotter, S., and Noel, J. *The Leadership Pipeline: How to Build the Leadership Powered Company*. (San Francisco, Jossey-Bass, 2001).

Chapter 2: Charting your course
1. Bennis, W. *Why Leaders Can't Lead: The Unconscious Conspiracy Continues*. (San Francisco, Jossey-Bass, 1989).
2. McCall, M. *The High Flyers: Developing the Next Generation of Leaders*. (Boston, Harvard Business School Press, 1998).

Chapter 3: Do you really know yourself?
1. Yu, D. *Confucius from the Heart: Ancient Wisdom for Today's World*. (London, Macmillan, 2009).

Chapter 4: What kind of leader do you wish to be?
1. Blake, R. and Mouton, J. *The Managerial Grid: Key Orientations for Achieving Production through People*. (Houston, Gulf Publishing Company,1968).

Chapter 5: Why EQ matters a great deal
1. Goleman, D. "What Makes a Leader," *Harvard Business Review* (November–December, 1998).

Chapter 6: Developing yourself
1. Kolb, D. *Experiential Learning: Experience as the Source of Learning and Development.* (New Jersey, Prentice Hall,1984).
2. McCall, M. "Leadership Development through Experience," *Academy of Management Executive* (Vol.18, No.3, 2004).

Chapter 7: Time management
1. Hallowell, D. "Overloaded Circuits: Why Smart People Underperform," *Harvard Business Review* (January, 2005).

Chapter 8: Leadership is a relationship
1. Coutu, D. "Smart Power: A Conversation with Leadership Expert Joseph S. Nye Jr.," *Harvard Business Review* (November, 2008).

Chapter 9: How to delegate
1. Landsberg, M. *The Tao of Coaching.* (London, Profile Books Ltd, 2003).
2. This concept is from Blanchard et al. on Situational Leadership.
3. Oncken, W.J. and Wass, D.L. "Management Time: Who's Got the Monkey?" *Harvard Business Review* (November-December, 1999).

Chapter 10: The Manager as coach
1. The GROW Model was developed by Graham Alexander in the 1980s.

Chapter 11: Coaching proficiencies
1. Nichols, M. *The Lost Art of Listening: How Learning to Listen Can Improve Relationships.* (New York, The Guilford Press, 1995).

Chapter 12: Giving feedback
1. Cannon, M.D. and Witherspoon, R. "Actionable Feedback: Unlocking the Power of Learning and Performance Improvement," *Academy of Management Executive* (Vol.19, No.2, 2005).
2. The www ebi approach came from Ng Nam Guan, a participant at a workshop that I conducted, during a discussion on how to give feedback.

Chapter 13: Asking for feedback
1. Advice from Marshall Goldsmith.

Chapter 14: Becoming a team leader
1. Wageman, R., Nunes, D.A., Burruss, J.A., and Hackman, J.R. *Senior Leadership Teams: What it Takes to Make Them Great.* (Boston, Harvard Business School Press, 2008).

Chapter 15: Forming and developing your team
1. Based on work on Blanchard et al. on Situation Team Leadership.
2. Siebdrat, F., Hoegl, M., and Ernst, H. "How to Manage Virtual Teams," *MITSloan Management Review* (Summer, 2009).

Chapter 16: Managing team dynamics

1. For more information, visit www.extendeddisc.com.
2. Belbin, M. *Team Roles at Work.* (London, Butterworth Heinemann, 2nd ed., 2010).

Chapter 17: The power of engagement

1. Much in this chapter has been based on the Towers Perrin 2007–2008 Global Workforce Study.

Chapter 18: Leveraging cultural diversity

1. The story about traffic congestion is based on: Tan, H.Y. "One Road to Safety Lies in Having Fewer Lines," *The Straits Times* (02 January, 2010).
2. Nisbett, R. *The Geography of Thought: How Asians and Westerners Think Differently ...and Why.* (New York, Free Press, 2003).

Chapter 19: Managing conflict

1. Edmondson, A.C., and Smith, D.M. "Too Hot to Handle? How to Manage Relationship Conflict," *California Management Review* (Fall 2006).

Chapter 20: Leading Change

1. I have drawn upon and adapted much from the work on leading change by various writers and thinkers such Bridges, Mitchell, Kotter et al.

Chapter 21: How to influence

1. I have drawn upon and adapted from the work on influencing by Conger, Cohen, Cialdini et al.

Chapter 22: Managing your boss

1. Gabarro, J.J. and Kotter, J.P. "Managing Your Boss," *Harvard Business Review* (June, 2005).

Chapter 23: Managing other stakeholders

1. Fischer, P. *The New Boss: How to Survive the First 100 Days.* (London, Kogan, 2007).

Chapter 24: Managing organizational politics

1. Reardon, K. *It's All Politics: Winning in a World where Hard Work and Talent aren't Enough.* (New York, Doubleday, 2005).

Chapter 25: The importance of self-renewal

1. Carpi, J. "Stress: It's Worse than You Think," *Psychology Today* (January-February, 1996).

Chapter 26: Your leadership journey

1. Heenan, D. *Double Lives: Crafting Your Life of Work and Passion for Untold Success* (Palo Alto, Davies-Black Publishing, 2002).

Appendix One: A coaching conversation
1. I would like to acknowledge Audrey Lee and Charles de Brabant for providing the context for this script.

Appendix Two: How bosses can facilitate successful transition for first-time managers
1. The "Leadership Turns Framework" has been adapted from the work of Charan, Drotter and Noel.

Appendix Three: Leveraging human capital for sustainable competitive advantage
1. McCall, M. "Leadership Development through Experience," *Academy of Management Executive* (Vol.18, No.3, 2004).

INDEX

ABOUT THE AUTHOR

BH Tan is one of Asia's leading executive coaches, leadership consultants and educators specializing in leadership development in a culturally-diverse environment. He is the president of Lead Associates (www.leadassociates.com.sg).

In the last 12 years, BH has worked with hundreds of senior executives in a wide range of industries. He has coached CEOs, presidents, VPs and middle managers in Asia, the United States and Europe, and top executive teams, to enhance their growth and effectiveness and bring greater value to their organizations. Leaders who have worked with BH Tan value his unique ability to provoke insightful perspectives arising from his practical and real world experience.

Prior to becoming an executive coach, BH was a senior business executive with 25 years of international leadership experience, working extensively in many parts of Asia, including various ASEAN countries, China, India, Taiwan, Korea, Japan as well as in the United States and Western Europe. He served at VP level in a number of well-known MNCs.

He has consulted with many leading international firms and organizations including AMD, L'Oreal, Dell, Johnson & Johnson, International Flavors & Fragrances, Microsoft, TSMC, BASF, Sanofi-Aventis, Exane Derivatives and Lafarge.

He lives in Singapore with his wife Boon Hwa and two daughters, Andrea and Amelia. He enjoys travelling, reading, jogging and listening to music.